T0158063

# Cooking with Kip

## A Cook's Memoir

KIP MEYERHOFF

# COOKING WITH KIP
## A COOK'S MEMOIR

iUniverse books may be ordered through booksellers or by contacting:

iUniverse
1663 Liberty Drive
Bloomington, IN 47403
www.iuniverse.com
1-800-Authors (1-800-288-4677)

ISBN: 978-1-4917-8202-6 (sc)
ISBN: 978-1-4917-8204-0 (e)

Library of Congress Control Number: 2015918225

Print information available on the last page.

iUniverse rev. date:    02/04/2016

Like *Macbeth*'s three witches, Kip cooks up a
caldron's stew of people, places, and things.
"Double, double toil and trouble,
Fire burn and caldron bubble."

# Contents

# Dedication

I knew little about being a father when I became one more than half a century ago. I believe this was true for my father too, and for his father. It's probably true for most new fathers. But we stumble along, learning as we go, hoping we're doing the right thing.

Charles Henry Meyerhoff was my father. He was a dangerous man, conflicted with vices and virtues. He had his code of loyalty to friends, a soft spot for the weak, and a belief that life should be lived. He raised a rebellious son who fled home as soon as he could, not because home was bad but because he could.

As the years passed, memories of my youth shed light on who I was. But the question of how I got to be me required me to cross the gulf that existed between me and my father, because there was no way he would make the first move.

And so it was our relationship was reestablished. Unfortunately this did not last but a few years, for wounds of the heart require much healing. Sadly, we were not on speaking terms at his death. Thus, I spent a decade seeking answers from family, friends, and foes—those he loved and those who loved him. It was worth all the effort, laughter, and tears, for to know my father is to know myself.

"Dad, how could two smart guys be so dumb?"

"I got you when you fell off the turnip truck"

# Foreword

Today is your lucky day. You hold a cookbook in your hands written by Kip Meyerhoff, a cook of great ability and knowledge, as we fans of his restaurant in Vevay, Indiana, will tell you.

The author is also an engaging writer with a lifetime of adventures in such exotic lands as Brooklyn, Hollywood, the Florida Keys, Korea, and, well, just about everywhere.

As a boy, Meyerhoff cooked pasta for wise guys at his father's New York hotel. He once made a Christmas breakfast for a house full of working girls in Seoul. He's as skilled at cooking exotic cuisine for fifty people as he is at preparing an intimate romantic dinner for two under moonlight.

Food, in its limitless variety, has been a constant love of this retired LAPD sergeant throughout his rich life, which has included shoot-outs in Watts, manhunts in Vegas, big-city bank robberies, and fistfights in the streets of Vevay.

The author has spent time with the famous (John Wayne, Ronald Reagan) as well as the infamous (Sonny Liston, Charles Manson), and he's brought back wonderful and inspired stories to amaze, delight, and educate.

Yes, today is your lucky day, and it's about to get even better. Turn the page, start reading, and get cooking.

Clay Warnick
Editor at the *River Times*

# Introduction

It goes without saying that youth is wasted on the young, and the winter of my years could be spent in bitter regret, thinking of wasted days and opportunities lost. The kindness of the forgetfulness of old age brings a smile to my face, as only the exceptional is now easily recalled. And so it is that my recollections are of the good times that made for a carefree youth, setting me apart from the real history of the '40s, '50s, and '60s. If I concentrate really hard, I can bring up images of painful events, but they are not clear; the voices are muted, and the colors are a whiter shade of pale. Nor can I hold on to these memories for more than a passing moment or two. But the good times are endless and vivid in my recollections, filled with faces flush with excitement, clear eyes, youthful bodies moving with grace, and a confidence born of ignorance of the fact that bad times might follow.

I'm glad to say that I spent most of my life living in the here and now. Little time was spent thinking of the consequence of each and every thing I said, did, or failed to do. I had places to go and people to see. I assumed that life would take care of itself, that good things were destined to happen for me, and that opportunities were always within reach. For me life is, was, and always will be about adventure!

The saying "You can't get there from here" assumes you know where you're going. Some have told me that they set out to get where they are today, overcoming obstacles, blocking out distractions, and focusing on purpose-driven lives. Well, good for them. For me there were no obstacles to overcome. There were a few challenges, for sure, but my goal was only to travel down life's road and enjoy the twists and turns, bumps and all. It was the journey that intrigued me, not what was waiting at the end of the road. During the trip, distractions were always welcomed, their entertainment value providing delight and relief from all those serious things that living confronts one with.

So, then, I recount past adventures here through the prism of a memory shaded and slightly bent by time and distance traveled. Those who believe hindsight is always twenty-twenty know not of human frailty. If these stories are not entirely accurate, they are surely how I wish to remember them. If you were there, please don't try to clarify my visions of the past. These are my memories; you are entitled to yours.

This is *Cooking with Kip*.

# Part 1

# *Learning to Cook*

# Chapter 1

## *A Life of Learning*

Dad taught me a lot of things, including that life is too short for cheap booze, tough steaks, or fast women. I caught on to the first two really quickly, but some lessons are best learned through experience. Of all the lessons he taught me, his lessons in the culinary arts served me best through my life's journey, although the pearl of wisdom about not drawing to inside straights probably saved me a fortune.

Dad's gourmand appetite provided me a culinary milieu in which to grow. A propensity for linear thought can be a one-way street to boredom, but the good Lord saw fit to wire me that way. Dad was similarly blessed (for you Darwinists out there). He was a color-blind math whiz; the numbers and chemistry of cooking intrigued him. Two tablespoons and two teaspoons, one-quarter cup or fourteen cups, a pinch of this, a dash of that—it was like reading the racing form for him. Salt-to-sugar ratios, volume to weight, heat to mass—these were mathematical equations telling him how long to roast a top round and at what temperature. The reasons why cake was not bread, why rice need not be bland, why green veggies should still be green when cooked—these were all chemical formulas to him.

He also taught me the axioms of cooking: a little sugar can go a long way; bitterness can spoil your appetite for life; tarts are not always a just dessert; heat can reduce heat; and hot is not always hot. The learning was fun, as much for me as for him, so when I showed an enthusiasm for the kitchen, he turned me over to a succession of hotel chefs to sate my curiosity.

Although technique and style varied widely, the science remained pretty constant, and as my knowledge grew, I felt free to experiment with presentation and taste. Dad firmly believed that if it looked good, it might taste better but that no amount of froufrou could help bad taste.

I won't shy away from the new as long as it falls within certain parameters. Celebrity chefs can be entertaining, but twelve inches of spun sugar on top of some ice cream rolled in crushed Oreos is not my idea of fine dining. So guys like Bobby Flay and Emeril and gals like Paula Dean and the Barefoot Contessa get my attention. They're putting out my kind of eats—wholesome food cooked right.

Applying the lessons I've learned has been an adventure. I hope my readers will pick up on some of these ideas.

# Chapter 2

## *Fire*

I remember an incident that occurred in my third June among humanity when I discovered fire. At the time I was not aware of the importance of this discovery, although I do recall a sixth-grade science teacher once telling us, "Man's discovery of fire led mankind out of the darkness to seek new adventures and eventually master the world." My discovery had a different result.

I was barely two and a half in June 1943. We lived in an old Victorian home on the banks of the Hudson River, somewhat similar to my current situation—a different house, different river, but eerily similar. I was an inquisitive youngster, always looking to explore the mysterious places and things found about the house. Not many boundaries had been set for me, mainly because I had yet to cross them. Except for being told where to go to the bathroom and not to go into my parents' room when the door was closed, I was free to follow my curiosity.

It was a sunny June day, as I recall. Mom specifically told me to play with my toys while she did the wash (my kids were told to watch TV), and so I pushed a toy truck around the kitchen floor until she took the wash outdoors to hang it on the line. I seized this opportunity to climb up on a chair to get at the cookie jar kept on the counter. Once I had the cookie population reduced by half, I spotted the box of Blue Diamond matches. As good as the cookie was, I put it down and grabbed the matches.

Wood-stick matches were a standard item in American households at this time in our history; there was usually a box by the stove, maybe one on the mantel. I'd watch with great interest the lighting of cigarettes, hoping I'd be allowed to blow the match out. Often the matches would be lit by striking the blue and white tips on the top of the stove, on the bricks of the fireplace, or on the bottom of a shoe to make fire. I once saw a man light a match with the seat of his pants, and my father could light one with the tip of his finger. Surely this was magic.

Seated on the rug in front of the stove, I proceeded to break a dozen or so matches in half, striking them on this and that. I remembered my mother using the side of the match box to light a match (Mom was a smart one for sure). Emulating Mom right down to the extended pinkie, I fired one up.

I held the burning match between my fingers, mesmerized by the flame. As the wood turned to ash, I discovered the flame could burn little boys' fingers and let it go with an "ouch" right into the open box from which it came!

I was amazed to see the box go up in a flash. Soon the rug caught on fire, and then the newspapers and kindling in the basket by the stove joined in. I panicked and let out a scream. "Mommy!"

"Kippy," she shouted as she rushed in the door, "what have you done?" She grabbed me by the hair on the top of my head and whisked me out the door. I watched excitedly as she dashed back in to battle the blaze. Using the kettle from the top of the stove, she extinguished the flames. The smoke and steam filled the kitchen, and the tears of a baby rolled down my fat cheeks. But I had discovered that water puts out fire. The thing about blisters was all new to me too, but I wasn't done "discovering" just yet.

When my father came home from a hard day of work, he found the doors and windows wide open, the kitchen a mess, and no supper to eat. When told his pride and joy almost burned down his house, he caused my arse to burn with the very hand that magically lit all those matches.

I often think of that incident, mostly when lighting my grill or the pilot on my stove. Now and then I'll burn a finger or two and hear my father's voice saying, "Don't play with fire, Son; you could get burned."

Did my fascination with fire lead to a lifetime of cooking? Searing and broiling, baking and boiling, sautéing and flambéing, roasting and toasting—I've done them all. Hot coals of charcoal, wood flames, gas, electricity, microwaves, and even infrared radiation have all put heat to my food. Did matches on a stove start me on this path?

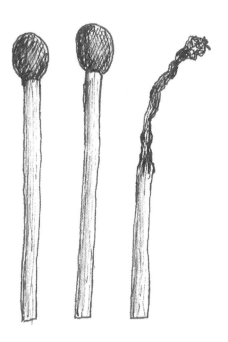

"One down—two to go."

# Chef's Notes:

_____

_____

_____

_____

_____

_____

_____

_____

_____

_____

_____

_____

_____

_____

_____

_____

_____

_____

_____

_____

Nellie Cassidy

# Chapter 3

## *My Hero*

Every time I roast a chicken, I think of Sunday dinners at my grandmother's. Stuffed, trussed, buttered, and seasoned, the freshly plucked bird would lay in a large roasting pan, surrounded by potatoes, carrots, onions, and parsnips to await the heat of the coal-burning oven.

When the time and temperature were just right, the lid would go on, and into the oven the roaster would go. Nanny would add more coal to the firebox. At the optimal moment, the lid would come off the roaster, and I would be given the task of basting, ladling pan juices over the bird with an ancient wooden spoon. I can still hear her voice cautioning, "Be quick about it, Kippy. You'll let all the heat out of my oven," the lilt of her Irish brogue music to my ears. Wonderful aromas would soon fill the house, letting all know it was time for Sunday dinner.

Nellie O'Shea arrived at Ellis Island during the early part of the second decade of the twentieth century. She made the nine-day journey from Ireland, drawn by the promise of marriage and a new life in America. Michael Cassidy had preceded his intended to America, leaving the "old sod" the year before. He met her at the gate, and they were soon married. Good Catholics, they brought four children into this world between 1915 and 1922.

All was good for the Cassidys as the twenties roared in, and all seemed possible until tragedy struck. Michael lost a leg in a work accident. Left crippled and mangled, he was never to work again. Thus it fell upon Nellie to become the breadwinner of the family.

These were not the times when married women with children entered the workforce. Untrained but undaunted, Nellie took her experience as a housewife and mother of four to the workplace. Her talent for cooking led to a job preparing meals for patients at the state hospital. When the resident physician tasted a patient's food that had been prepared by Nellie, he pulled her out of the mess hall and installed her as cook for the medical staff.

In spite of all her prayers and novenas and the candlelit icons in every room of their house, Michael died, leaving Nellie to do it all. Grief and hardship could not get her down, and bitterness was not let in the door. Her faith unshaken, she persisted. She never drove a car and couldn't afford one if she could. She bicycled over three miles to work, rain or shine, walking through the snow when the bike wouldn't go; she worked to feed her family and to put clothes on their backs and a roof over their heads.

Nellie got her children through school, not letting even the Great Depression slow her down. She saw her daughter marry. She sent her sons off to war, and her prayers brought them home. She doted over eight grandchildren, never missing a birthday and giving them "a little something" for Christmas too. This great lady did all this while working at the same hospital for over thirty years. No need to ask who my hero is.

My grandmother kept a flock of layers in a coop out back until the war ended in '45. I was five years old when all my uncles returned home from their service to our country. Although the end of rationing meant fresh eggs could now be had at the market, the celebratory dinners marking the return of each of her three sons were the real reason her flock was reduced to zero.

One of my memories of those times is of a tree stump in Nellie's backyard and the sharp hatchet protruding from it. They were used to dispatch all those poor birds. I also remember a large kettle of boiling water on an open fire for plucking the chickens and burning off pin feathers. In fact, the smell of wet feathers still conjures up visions of headless chickens flapping around the yard in search of their heads.

## Nellie's Roasted Chicken

For best results, use a large roasting pan with a rack and domed lid. I highly recommend brining your bird by soaking it overnight in a solution of one cup kosher salt with one gallon of water.

Ingredients:
1 fat hen, 3 to 3 1/2 pounds
1 stick of butter
2 cups chicken stock or water
1 tablespoon kosher salt
1 tablespoon fresh ground pepper
1 tablespoon dried sage leaves

*Bouquet*
1 bunch fresh parsley
1 bunch carrot tops
1 celery root
1 large Spanish onion, quartered

*Vegetables*
potatoes, carrots, onions, parsnips

Preheat oven to 425 degrees F.

Rinse the chicken and thoroughly pat dry with paper towels. Place bird on nonporous, clean surface and rub inside and out with softened butter. Season with salt, pepper, and sage.

Stuff the bird with the bouquet. Place seasoned bird on rack, breast side up, and roast uncovered 35–40 minutes, allowing bird to brown.

Arrange potatoes, carrots, onions, and parsnips around bottom of pan. Pour in two cups of chicken stock, cover with lid and place on middle rack of oven. Bake at 375 degrees F for 45 minutes.

Remove lid and continue to cook, basting frequently with pan juices, for 20 more minutes.

Remove from oven and let bird rest on serving platter for 15–20 minutes before carving.

Meanwhile, make a gravy with the pan juices.

Vegetables will be well done, stew-like, and buttery. Yum!

# Chapter 4

## *Bookie Cookie*

It is my hope that readers of this effort might be inspired to allow their kids to learn what it takes to navigate a kitchen, steer a stove, and appreciate the efforts of others trying to provide for them. It's the old "feed them a fish or teach them how to fish" argument.

I could wash a dish from the time I was five and never thought of reporting my parents for violating child labor laws. Getting ready for school, I could open a box of Wheaties, pour milk and juice, toast bread, and stack dirty dishes in the sink to await my return. These early lessons in self-reliance have served me well over the years.

My father began my real cooking lessons when I was but seven. Dad received his formal training in the culinary arts while doing a stretch "upstate," thanks to the efforts of New York's Governor Tom Dewey. While "up the river," Dad prepared thousands of meals for some of the toughest food critics ever assembled.

While answering calls in a phone bank with a couple of his cohorts in his lucrative bookmaking operation and awaiting the results from Aqueduct, Saratoga, or Pimlico, Dad would instruct me in the preparation of that evening's dinner fare. By the time I was eight, I knew the difference between braising and broiling, baking and boiling. I also knew the difference between the daily double and a three-horse parlay.

One of my first cooking lessons required a dozen eggs, an egg cup, a toaster, a loaf of bread, and a saucepan with water. What I thought was going to be a lesson on how to boil eggs was really, like most things in life, a lesson about timing. He made me a breakfast of a perfect, soft-boiled egg and hot buttered toast, and after I ate, he had me make breakfast for him. Six eggs and five slices of burnt toast later, my inner clock worked. The following two recipes might be a way to start your kids on the path to self-reliance.

## Cheesy Soup

This soup selection is a combination of two kid favorites: boxed macaroni and cheese and canned tomato soup. Have your young ones follow the stove-top directions for each and then combine them just before serving. Sprinkle a little shredded cheddar on top to "kick it up a notch!"

## The King's Sandwich

This grilled peanut-butter-and-banana goodie was Elvis Presley's favorite. You'll need a large nonstick frying pan, a little butter, and some slices of white bread.

Peel a banana, slice it in half lengthwise, and then cut each strip in half crossways.

Fit a couple of pieces of banana on one slice of bread, spread peanut butter on another slice of bread and press the two halves of bread together to make the sandwich.

Melt some butter in the pan and grill to desired doneness. Flip to do other side.

Instead of trying to explain Elvis or why he was "the King," play "Hound Dog" or "Blue Suede Shoes" for them while they eat the King's favorite.

The C.I. Hotel, circa 1958

# Chapter 5

## *The Hotel*

I grew up in a New York hotel my father owned. Forty rooms, a bar and grill, a full-service restaurant, and a couple of banquet rooms kept the employees jumping around the clock. The cast of characters that came and went were right out of a Damon Runyon novel. My father believed in diversity and believed that my exposure to the good, the bad, and the ugly would help my travels along life's many paths.

By the time Dad got into the hotel business, I was already schooled in cooking basics. Our first chef at the hotel was a Chinese man who hardly spoke English. Since Dad didn't speak any Chinese, he hired the chef's teenage son to bus tables and assist his father. This arrangement lasted for four years until the son graduated from high school and joined the navy. The next chef arrived from Germany. Since he didn't cook Chinese, the new menu featured schnitzel, potato pancakes, and red cabbage, but I mostly ate the apple strudel. He liked to cook with schnapps—not that he put it in the food—so he was replaced by a little old lady from Naples. She had little use for English and insisted that Dad hire her son to run the kitchen. Thankfully, Ozzie could cook.

There was also a fill-in chef from Hungary, but the most foreign to me was a Dixie boy from South Carolina. I assumed he was always in a cheerful mood because when he wasn't talking, he'd be whistling.

Although I knew most of his tunes, it was three months before I could make out what he was saying and six months before I understood what it meant. But he made the best fried chicken I have ever eaten!

## The Dixie Whistler's Fried Chicken

Ingredients:
2 (3-pound) fryer chickens, cut up
1 quart buttermilk
2 cups all-purpose flour
4 large eggs, beaten
2 cups fine bread crumbs
1 tablespoon salt

1/4 teaspoon each black pepper, white pepper, mustard powder, paprika, and onion powder
2 slices bacon
4 cups shortening

In a large bowl, cover chicken with buttermilk and marinate for 90 minutes at room temperature.

Place flour on a plate.

On another plate, mix bread crumbs, salt, black pepper, white pepper, mustard powder, paprika, and onion powder.

Place beaten eggs in a bowl.

Remove chicken from buttermilk, shaking excess liquid from chicken pieces, and dredge in flour. Dip floured pieces in beaten egg, and then coat with bread crumbs.

Heat 3 cups of shortening in a large, heavy skillet to about 350 degrees F. You'll need about 1/2 inch of shortening to properly cook the chicken, adding more shortening as you go.

Add bacon slices and cook until crisp. Remove the bacon.

Starting with the largest pieces, add chicken to bacon flavored shortening. Don't overcrowd. Turn chicken pieces with tongs to brown lightly and evenly and parcook (10–15 minutes). Drain on paper towel and let cool to room temp before refrigerating, if desired.

Finish cooking chicken by deep-frying at 400 degrees F for 5–7 minutes, depending on size (more time for breasts, less time for wings), or by baking at 350 degrees F for 15–20 minutes.

Serve with mashed potatoes, steamed carrots, buttermilk biscuits, and a glass of sweetened tea. This is good, and I'm not just whistling Dixie!

### Chicken Gravy

Ingredients:
1/2 stick butter
1/2 cup finely diced onion
2 tablespoons flour
1 cup chicken stock
a pinch of dried sage
a few drops of hot sauce
2 tablespoons half-and-half or cream
1 tablespoon chopped fresh parsley
salt and pepper to taste

Melt butter in small saucepan over medium heat.

Add onion and sauté for 5 minutes.

Stir in flour and cook 2 minutes more.

Whisk in stock, sage, and hot sauce and simmer 4–5 minutes to thicken.

Stir in cream and parsley. Taste and adjust seasoning.

Eat your vegetables.

# Chef's Notes:

_____
_____
_____
_____
_____
_____
_____
_____
_____
_____
_____
_____
_____
_____
_____
_____
_____
_____
_____
_____
_____

I

## Chapter 6

## *Roxano's Restaurant*

I purchased a restaurant with my sweetheart's blessing over twenty years ago. It was a modest enterprise with excellent potential that the sellers hadn't been able to realize because of owner fatigue. I knew most of what I needed to know to reach this potential because of what my father taught me.

Over the years that followed, Linda and I worked hard, made some money, and enjoyed success. Most of our decisions were the right ones, and most of the decisions that went wrong were not *our* decisions at all. They were mine.

Although the financial rewards have been good, the other rewards have been more gratifying. Sure it's about the food, but it's also about the people.

Foremost was the community of Vevay, which has supported us faithfully, forgiven our mistakes, and championed our efforts. They have provided us with a trainable workforce willing to adopt the "Roxano's Way." The result was good food and good service, two of the three cornerstones of a successful restaurant. The third pillar for our continued success is reasonable pricing.

Reasonable pricing is dependent on ingredient quality, so our first rule was "never compromise quality to save a buck," as my father put it. We live by this rule. I spent considerable time negotiating with vendors to keep costs as low as possible. Quality—that's what our customers are entitled to expect for their money. They don't say "Let's go to Roxano's; the food's cheap." They say "Let's go to Roxano's; the food's good!"

Now that I have identified the three pillars of success and given you the rule about never compromising quality, you should be ready to go into the restaurant business. Oh yeah, you should also know how to cook, manage people, budget, fill out twelve tax reports per month, comply with all the health and safety laws, write a menu, and fill out reports for a dozen government entities that could care less if you succeed or fail. No wonder three out of four new restaurants fail within five years.

There is an argument among pizzeria owners: Is it the dough or is it the sauce? Truthfully, it depends, because ultimately the customer determines what sells and what doesn't. If a proprietor doesn't cater to his customers' tastes, he will not succeed.

When I make pizza at home, the sauce is different from the sauce I made at my restaurants, where I sold hundreds of thousands of pizzas. The

secret here is in the proportions and the quality
of each ingredient.

Here is a list of ingredients for pizza sauce:

olive oil
crushed and peeled plum tomatoes
salt
garlic
onion
basil
oregano
red pepper flakes
fennel

Basic pizza dough is much like white bread
with a little less leavening agent and a bit more
flavoring. Again, ingredient quality is paramount.

Here are the ingredients for pizza dough:

active dry yeast
warm water
flour
kosher salt
white pepper
olive oil

At home I'll add some dried herbs, like rosemary, basil, and oregano, to make a focaccia crust. Knead in a couple of tablespoons of grated Parmesan and substitute a few ounces of beer for a few ounces of water, and you might be ready for a pizza contest.

One of my favorite pizzas is the focaccia crust sauced with a garlicky white pizza sauce and topped with slices of herb-roasted chicken and bits of crumbled bacon. Although the classic pizza is topped with mozzarella, I prefer shredded Asiago on this baby.

Garlic-roasted shrimp splashed with a few drops of Tabasco go great on a white pizza, but I eliminate the cheese topping when I make this one.

## Garlicky White Pizza Sauce

Ingredients:
2 tablespoons butter
1 teaspoon minced garlic
2 tablespoons all-purpose flour
1 cup half-and-half
1/4 teaspoon kosher salt
1/4 teaspoon white pepper

1/2 teaspoon dried basil leaves
1/2 cup shredded Parmesan

Melt butter in a 1-quart saucepan over medium heat. Add garlic and sauté for 1 minute.

Whisk in flour one tablespoon at a time. Cook while stirring for 2 minutes.

Heat half-and-half in microwave for 1 minute. Slowly whisk warmed cream into the butter and flour mixture and continue to cook until mixture thickens.

Slowly stir in cheese and allow to melt.

Remove from heat. Sauce is ready to use.

# Chapter 7

## *Continuing Education*

"Believing you know it all is either delusional or a good indication of your ignorance." That's one of those pearls of wisdom Dad dropped on me in my teens. The culinary arts continue to evolve based on new technologies, science, and the creativity of chefs around the world.

Much of what I know about cooking was taught to me in a variety of kitchens by people who had a similar passion for good eating. I was made familiar with haute cuisine by a father who insisted I be exposed to foie gras in the finest French restaurants New York could offer. The thought of goose liver spiked with cognac was difficult for a sixteen-year-old cooking enthusiast to wrap his mind around, but a pâté seemed like just another form of liverwurst. Yet the classic haute foie gras is so much more, requiring many hours of preparation and special handling.

I think this is one of the things that caused Auguste Escoffier, the famous "Chef of Kings and King of Chefs," to start a culinary revolution more than a century ago. His ideas of fresher, lighter, less-cooked dishes, seasoned to enhance the natural flavors of ingredients rather than mask them, was new to the culinary world. His development of innovative cooking techniques soon caught on throughout Europe and then to America. He was the world's first celebrity chef.

Chef Paul Bocuse, acclaimed "Chef of the Century," continued the development of nouvelle cuisine as more an evolution of than a rebellion against the old ways. Fortunately, the teachings of both these world-renowned chefs are being passed on to aspiring chefs around the world in culinary schools that bear their names. Their books have sold millions of copies worldwide. Two of Paul Bocuse's many books, *Professional Chef* and *Professional Chef Study Guide* should be read by anyone seriously considering a culinary career.

There are hundreds of culinary-arts schools in this great country of ours, new ones opening each week. Many colleges and universities now offer certificates and degrees in food-service management; hotel, restaurant, and hospitality management; and diet and nutrition. Yet, even a degree is no guarantee of success.

However, all would benefit from a few years of apprenticeship under a mentor who respects those who feed us. All chefs know: *no farms, no food!*

## Perfect Boiled Eggs

I can thank my father for having at least one thing in common with the great chefs Bocuse and Escoffier. Dad taught me how to boil an egg while explaining the nuances of timing.

The answer to the question *How much time does it takes to boil an egg?* is quite simple: It depends! Chicken eggs are sized as small, medium, large, and extra large. The bigger the egg, the more time it takes to properly cook.

Another variable is altitude. Water boils at 212 degrees F at sea level but ten degrees cooler in the Mile High City. The lower the temperature, the more cooking time. Eggs right out of the refrigerator require more time than eggs at room temperature. The following guide works for room-temperature eggs, close to sea level.

Place eggs in saucepan and cover with 1 inch of cold tap water. Place over medium-high heat and bring to a boil, uncovered.

Remove from heat, cover, and let stand for 1 1/2–2 minutes for soft or 12–13 minutes for hard.

Rinse under running tap water to stop the cooking. Enjoy a perfect egg.

**Chef's Notes:**

"People not lost in the crowd"

# Part 2

# *People*

# Chapter 8

## *Chef Wu*

It was another rainy New York afternoon as we stood under the roof of the station platform waiting for the train to roll to a stop. Dad and I were there to meet a new employee hired through a mob-controlled union. John Wu stood all of five feet six and probably weighed 145 pounds in his suit if he were carrying a lot of change. His jet-black hair was slicked back under a grey fedora; twinkling ebony eyes peeked out from under the brim. A Fu Manchu accented thin lips that seemed to frown. *My God*, I thought, *my father has hired Charlie Chan to be his* Chef de Hotel!

Nineteen fifty-two was a pivotal year in my upbringing. My father and his partners had purchased a one-hundred-year-old hotel, bar, and restaurant where we now lived. I was to spend a large portion of my teen years, at my father's insistence, working in Chef Wu's kitchen. Dad had been giving me cooking lessons since I was seven, but now he was turning my culinary education over to Chef Wu, whose English was so bad that his son was brought in from Texas to wait tables and interpret.

I, like most, did what my father wanted, even though I would much rather have been out running the streets with my friends. Curiosity made me a precocious student, but Chef Wu's teaching methods were as strange to me as the Chinese characters labeling stores in the kitchen's larder. So on day one, I reported to the kitchen for the school after school.

Pointing to a very large cleaver resting on a cutting board the chef said, "No touch-ee." He then pointed to a large wok and a curved metal spatula and said, "You wash-ee." I took the items to the sink and, employing my six years of dish-washing experience, returned the implements to him well washed and dried.

He nodded and placed the wok on a high flame and said, "You watch-ee." He splashed some peanut oil in the wok, waited for it to heat, then added a large scoop of cold cooked rice. It sizzled and popped while he noisily moved it around the wok with his spatula. When it started to produce a nutlike fragrance and a little color, he amazed me by sliding the frying rice up the sides of the wok and made it stay there, leaving the bottom of the wok exposed.

A few drops of sesame oil were joined by a pinch of sesame seeds and about a half-cup of diced roast pork. He gently moved this around for thirty seconds without disturbing the clinging rice, allowing the seeds to toast. Next he added a handful of mixed raw vegetables that included some mushrooms, bean sprouts, green onion, shredded carrot, and slivers of water chestnuts. A pour of soy sauce preceded some serious woking with the rice.

Chef Wu pushed the mixture back up the sides of the wok, added a little oil to the bare bottom, and scrambled up an egg. When it set, he incorporated it into the rice. He plated up his Cantonese Fried Rice, stuck two chopsticks in it, and handed it to me, saying, "Eat."

The fried rice was great, but this day's lesson wasn't anywhere near done. As I finished my after school snack, he wiped out the wok with a clean towel and put it back on the fire. "You make-ee," he said. "Me eat."

Here was my chance to show the chef my skills. I made the fried rice just like Chef Wu, but when it came time for the plating, I just had to add some of my own moves to the process. As the wok started to slip off the burner I grabbed for the handle like a cat. Four-hundred-degree wok handles are difficult to hold, and the wok hit the floor like a bomb, the contents flying like shrapnel. I let out a howl and ran for the cold water. As I let the water cool my burned and blistered fingers, Chef Wu pointed to the mess all over his kitchen floor and said, "You clean-ee!" So at my first day at Chinese cooking school, I learned that woks are hot, that we clean as we go, and that I really like Cantonese Fried Rice.

My education was to continue for the next few years. I learned that Wu came to America during the roaring twenties, settling in San Francisco with relatives. An arranged marriage resulted in two children, who were raised in Texas as the chef worked restaurants in California, San Antonio, and New York. I always believed he knew more English than he let on. Although his son and daughter were raised in America, they always spoke in Cantonese to their father, and he to them. He worked at the hotel for five years, retiring when his son joined the navy. He was a great cook.

Pork, poultry, and fish were the main staples of Chinese restaurants throughout America in the '50s, and the most popular item on the hotel menu was Chef Wu's Chinese Roast Spareribs. As a kid, my experience with spareribs was limited to the German version cooked in kraut or my Nanny Nellie's boiled Irish version with cabbage and potatoes, both of which I could never get enough of until Southern BBQ came into my life.

Chef Wu would start out with three or four full slabs of ribs sawed in half lengthwise. He trimmed them and rubbed them with a dry mix of spices and brown sugar before slow roasting the pork. After a couple of hours, he would turn and baste the racks every ten to fifteen minutes until he was satisfied that the ribs were done to perfection.

In the following version I've modified the recipe by substituting back ribs for spareribs and five-spice powder for all the spices Chef Wu used for his rub. But authentic flavor cannot be attained without using three key ingredients: five-spice powder, sesame oil, and hoisin sauce.

## Chef Wu's Chinese Roast Ribs

Ingredients:
1 (2-pound) rack baby back ribs
1 cup soy sauce
1/2 cup rice wine vinegar

*Dry Rub*
1/2 cup brown sugar
1 tablespoon five-spice powder
1 teaspoon salt
1/2 teaspoon white pepper
1/2 teaspoon garlic powder

*Basting Sauce*
1 tablespoon freshly grated ginger
1/2 cup honey
4 tablespoons sesame oil
4 tablespoons hoisin sauce
4 tablespoons soy sauce
1 teaspoon red food coloring

Cut rack of ribs into two-rib pieces and place in gallon-size food bag. Add soy sauce and vinegar. Seal the bag tightly and refrigerate 4 hours or longer, turning bag a few times to evenly marinate the ribs. Remove ribs and discard marinade.

Preheat oven to 300 degrees F.

Mix up ingredients for the dry rub and apply evenly to all surfaces of the ribs.

Line a baking pan with foil and arrange ribs, meat side down, so the pieces don't touch. Cover with foil and tightly seal the pan. Bake 90 minutes.

While ribs bake, mix together ingredients for the basting sauce.

Remove ribs from oven and uncover. Turn ribs meat side up and baste. Return to a 350 degree F oven and roast ribs another hour, basting every 10 minutes.

I enjoy these succulently sweet and spicy ribs with Cantonese fried rice and Szechuan green beans. Unsweetened hot tea is my beverage of choice, but a cold Chinese beer works well too.

Chef Wu kept a kitchen garden during the five summers he worked at the hotel. He grew herbs, peppers, eggplant, and the foot-long green beans he used in the following recipe. He would parcook his fresh beans in the deep fryer for 2 minutes before they hit his wok. Here I've substituted parboiling, which is longer than a quick blanching.

## Szechuan Green Beans

Ingredients:
1 pound fresh green beans
1/2 teaspoon red pepper flakes
2 tablespoons canola oil, divided
1 teaspoon minced garlic
1 teaspoon grated fresh ginger
1 teaspoon sesame oil
1 tablespoon soy sauce
1 tablespoon hoisin sauce
1/4 teaspoon toasted sesame seeds

Parboil beans in salted water 4 minutes. Immediately remove and plunge beans into an ice bath to stop the cooking and keep a bright green color.

Heat wok over medium-high heat and toast red pepper flakes for 1 minute.

Add 1 tablespoon canola oil, garlic, and ginger and sauté an additional minute.

Add beans, remaining canola oil, and sesame oil and stir-fry until color starts to appear (4 minutes).

Add rest of ingredients and continue stir-frying 3 minutes, coating the beans.

This makes a great side dish for any pork dish. You may wish to substitute broccoli florets for the beans. They are equally enjoyable.

By adding thin slices of grilled steak or roasted chicken breast during the final step, you create a main-course stir-fry to be served over steamed rice or tossed with rice noodles. Chef Wu would surely approve.

## Asian Cucumber Salad

The following chilled side salad makes a nice accompaniment to any of these delicious meals. Since Asia is such a big place, I've included a couple of variations. Mix and match ingredients as your taste buds dictate.

Ingredients:
1 cucumber, peeled, cut lengthwise, seeded, and cut into 1/8-inch slices
2 green onions, chopped

1/4 cup water

4 tablespoons rice wine vinegar

1 tablespoon sugar

1 teaspoon salt

1/2 teaspoon sesame oil

1/4 teaspoon toasted sesame seeds

Combine all the ingredients. Cover and refrigerate before serving.

Variations include adding some grated fresh ginger, red pepper flakes, fresh lime juice, fresh cilantro, chopped roasted peanuts, sliced jalapenos, radishes or water chestnuts, minced garlic, and, of course, soy sauce. Now you're cooking with Kip.

# Chef's Notes:

# Chapter 9

## *Capo di*

Once upon a time, in my formative years during the midfifties, there was a small restaurant in New York's Little Italy named the Capuzzelle di Agnello. The translation from the Italian would be the Lamb's Head, and this was one of the features of their menu. The first time I saw the presentation of their featured dish, I was struck by the realization that no amount of garlic, wine reduction, savory herbs, or spices could get me to eat something that was staring at me. But this was where I was introduced to gnocchi, those little Italian potato dumplings cooked and served like a pasta dish.

As I recall, Ozzie Atourino, my dad's *chef de hotel*, brought me to the restaurant because the Broadway crowd favored the place and a number of Italian actors, who Ozzie knew, were expected after the show.

My father's hotel was in its Italian phase at this time, and Ozzie's celebrity status gained us access to the kitchen. Most of the conversation was in Italian except when it was directed at me. I asked Vincenzo what all the potatoes were doing in an Italian kitchen. It was then I learned of gnocchi and was given a quick primer in its making.

About that time, a commotion in the dining room signaled the arrival of Ben Gazzara and Harry Guardino to the "Capo di." They were with a few cast members of *Hat Full of Rain* which was enjoying a very successful run starring Tony Franciosa. These were all New York guys enjoying the cheers and adulation of the neighborhood in a time devoid of paparazzi, when you could walk the streets, take a train, or window-shop without your privacy being disturbed.

Since these were meat-and-pasta guys, we enjoyed a family-style Italian feast that showcased the gnocchi served with roasted leg of lamb in a wine sauce laced with herbs and garlic. Bottles of Chianti adorned the table, and we finished with desserts of cannoli pastries and cups of espresso spiked with anisette. What could be better?

# Gnocchi

This recipe is a reasonable shortcut to making gnocchi. I've substituted an instant mashed potato mix for potatoes to save the work of peeling, boiling, ricing, and cooling a couple of pounds of real spuds. But if you have an extra hour to spend in your kitchen, give the real thing a shot.

Ingredients:
1 cup instant mashed potato mix
1 cup boiling water
1 tablespoon butter
1 egg, beaten
1 teaspoon salt
a dash or two of white pepper
1 1/2 cups flour

Put potato flakes in a mixing bowl. Add butter and pour in boiling water. Mix well and let potato mixture cool.

Stir in beaten egg, salt, and pepper. Slowly add a little over one cup of the flour, mixing and folding dough.

Place dough on floured dough board. Knead and add small amounts of flour until mixture holds its shape but is not too stiff.

Divide dough into thirds and form each part into a ropelike shape about as thick as your finger.

Using a sharp knife, cut dough ropes into 3/4-inch pieces. Press each piece with fork tines to about half their original thickness. (The resulting ridges are great for holding your sauce on the dumpling.)

Bring 3 quarts of salted water to a boil in pasta pot and add a third of the gnocchi to the boiling water. Using a slotted spoon, remove cooked dumplings as they float to the top. Place in a warmed dish. Repeat until all are done.

## Gnocchi with Gorgonzola Sauce

Ingredients:
2 green onions, chopped
1/2 stick butter, divided
4 tablespoons flour
1 cup light cream
6 ounces crumbled Gorgonzola cheese
1/4 teaspoon fresh ground black pepper
4 cups gnocchi

fresh parsley for garnish

In 1-quart saucepan, melt 2 tablespoons of butter over medium heat. Add chopped onions and sauté 2 minutes.

Add remaining butter and melt. Slowly stir in flour to thicken.

Stir in cream and bring to a simmer, being careful not to scald or boil.

Stir in cheese crumbles, stirring to blend. Season sauce with fresh ground pepper.

Pour sauce over gnocchi and garnish with parsley.

Serve as a side to your favorite seasoned cut of meat, or as a main dish with a salad and garlic bread. Perhaps have lime sherbet, drizzled with an orange liqueur, and an anisette cookie for dessert. Oh boy!

## Fried Gnocchi with Parmesan

The versatility of these little dumplings makes them a cook's friend. Gnocchi, like most pastas, are great with a good tomato sauce and also work well in a soup. I like buttered gnocchi as a side with veal scaloppini, but I am really fond of deep-fried gnocchi.

Ingredients:
2 cups fresh gnocchi
1/2 cup freshly grated Parmesan cheese
1/4 teaspoon salt
1 quart canola oil for frying

Heat oil in 2-quart saucepan to 360 degrees F.

Cooking in batches, half a cup at a time, fry the gnocchi to a light golden brown. They will float to the top when cooked (about 3 minutes).

Remove with slotted spoon to a paper-towel-lined cookie sheet to drain.

Sprinkle with salt, toss with cheese, and enjoy.

**Chef's Notes:**

_____

_____

_____

_____

_____

_____

_____

_____

_____

_____

_____

_____

_____

_____

_____

_____

_____

_____

_____

_____

_____

_____

# Chapter 10

## *The Sicilian Hit Man*

In the late sixties, my grade-school-age children were enjoying life in suburban Los Angeles. They had a backyard full of pets, including a cat and a dog, rabbits, pigeons, and a California tortoise named Tuffy. One Easter their mother and I saw no particular reason not to buy them each a cute and fluffy baby chick.

Shortly after the holiday passed and the lure of Easter candy had faded, my children learned that cats eat birds, and soon there was only one baby chick, whose fluffy yellow plumes were rapidly changing to a mass of white spikes. (This hairdo seemed appropriate for the late sixties.) Although my two boys were quickly bored with baby chicks, my daughter was sure that the sole survivor was indeed hers. I must confess the bird's ability to escape the jaws of death surprised me, and as spring turned to summer, the fluffy little chick turned into a full-grown rooster that spent most of his day atop the back of our California tortoise, who seemed to enjoy giving the bird a ride!

Roosters are mean and noisy animals. As a city boy, this fact had not previously occurred to me. But by July, we knew that if we didn't put the rooster in the pigeon coop at night, we would receive a bunch of telephone calls the next morning from irate neighbors awakened at dawn by a crescendo of cock-a-doodle-doos.

Returning home in the wee hours of a hot August night (after the party hearty), I was in no shape for a rooster roundup. I told the missus that I would put the chicken in the coop at first light. Two hours later, my dreams were interrupted by a couple of elbow jabs to my ribs. Wifey was reminding me of the impending phone calls if I failed to deliver on my promise. Thus, I staggered into the backyard with a slice of bread in one hand and a broom in the other in search of Mr. Rooster.

My plan was simple: coax the bird into the coop with the bread and fend off any attack with the broom. As dawn cracked, the rooster crowed, and I tossed the bread into the coop. Ignoring my offering, the bird rushed me like the proverbial bat out of hell. As I parried his wing thrusts with the broom, I discovered our dog had preceded me into the yard to do his morning business. The warmth of that business gushed between my toes as the bird mocked me with clucks and crows.

At that stage of my life, I was a briefs man; boxers arrived in my thirties. Enraged by my situation and desiring to take it out on the chicken, I chased the bird with my trusty broom and a flow of expletives. It was then that I noticed my neighbor peering over the fence. Realizing what my neighbor was witnessing, I beat a hasty retreat into the house. We didn't get a Christmas card from this neighbor that year. I don't know if it was because of the rooster or because I set his house on fire with celebratory fireworks during my previous New Year's Eve party.

While washing the dog stuff from my foot, I hatched a plot to get rid of the bird. Again, it was a simple plan: while we took the kids to the local pancake house for Sunday brunch, my Sicilian father-in-law would off the bird. Our cover story would be that Mr. Rooster had run off in search of a hen. That evening, after the deed was done, we went to Grandma's for Sunday dinner.

"How did you get those scratches on your face, Grandpa?" my daughter asked across the table.

"Helping Grandma fix dinner!" he replied, a wry smile on his face.

## Cock-a-Doodle Cacciatore

Cacciatore is a time-honored cooking technique that will make any mean bird palatable, even this one.

Ingredients:
1 large chicken cut into 8 parts—2 thighs, 2 drumsticks, 2 wings, and 2 breasts (save back, neck, liver, gizzard, and heart for your stockpot)
1 tablespoon salt
1 tablespoon pepper
3/4 cup flour
1/2 cup olive oil
1 large bell pepper, diced
1 large onion, diced
2 cloves garlic, peeled and minced
1 cup red wine
1 (28-ounce) can plum tomatoes in juice

1 (14-ounce) can chicken stock
1 teaspoon dried basil
1 teaspoon dried oregano
1/2 cup fresh Italian parsley

Season chicken pieces with salt and pepper. Dredge chicken in flour and place on plate.

Heat oil in large skillet over medium-high heat. Brown chicken pieces on all sides. Remove chicken to plate.

Discard half the oil from pan. Sauté peppers and onions in remaining oil for 3–4 minutes. Add minced garlic and cook an additional minute.

Add wine and deglaze pan. Add tomatoes with juice and dried herbs. Bring to a simmer while breaking up tomatoes with spoon.

Add chicken back into pan along with stock. Simmer uncovered over medium heat for 35–40 minutes, allowing sauce to thicken. Meat should be ready to fall from the bones.

Serve in bowls over your favorite pasta, garnished with parsley.

A salad and some garlic bread complete the meal. The wine you made the sauce with would be perfect to drink.

## Aunt Rose's Garlic Bread

Ingredients:
1 stick butter
4 tablespoons extra-virgin olive oil
2 cloves garlic, peeled and pressed
1 loaf French bread, cut lengthwise
1 teaspoon fresh rosemary leaves, chopped

Melt butter in oil in small saucepan over medium heat. Sauté garlic until fragrant.

Spoon butter mixture onto loaf halves. Sprinkle on rosemary, and toast under broiler.

Cut into 2-inch pieces, and serve warm in a bread basket.

# Chef's Notes:

_____
_____
_____
_____
_____
_____
_____
_____
_____
_____
_____
_____
_____
_____
_____
_____
_____
_____
_____
_____
_____

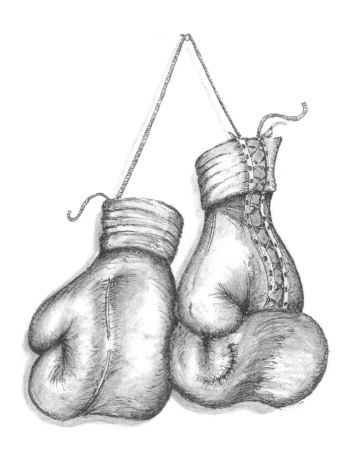

# Chapter 11

## *The Champ*

Joe Louis was not the giant I'd thought he would be. His robe hung loosely from his shoulders, and his back was not the width I'd been expecting. When he turned to face us, his smile did not hide the sadness in his eyes, and his thin mustache implied a frown his lips could not erase.

This was not Joe Louis, heavyweight champion of the world, the first Negro athlete to transcend race, the true American hero, the destroyer of Nazi myth, the man who'd sold millions of war bonds, the man who'd served in his country's military, and the reigning world champ from before my birth to well into my grade school years. No, this was Joe Louis the wrestler, a broken man, hounded by our government for taxes owed on money he never saw.

The New York State Athletic Commission appointed officials as part of a patronage system that the government had been refining since the war—the Revolutionary War. I was brought to the arena by an acquaintance of my father. He had been assigned to referee the matches and see that all the rules were followed. Since winners were determined by contractual agreement and a promoter's script, the referee was merely part of the show's choreography.

To compensate the promoter for my free pass, I was made to sell mimeographed programs for a quarter, dutifully hawking in the aisles with "Program here! Get your program here!" When my allotment of programs was almost gone, the ref escorted me to the dressing room to meet the wrestlers. I was ushered into the champ's presence, and introductions were made.

"Hi, kid," he said, extending his large, gnarly hand, which made mine disappear.

"Kip," I croaked, thinking he misheard my name. I handed him a pen and program, which he signed without enthusiasm. I thanked his back as he resumed his conversation with Antonino Argentina Rocca and the rest of the performers.

After the show ended and the referee was paid, the ref drove me back to my father's hotel and dropped me off. The bouncer told me that Dad was in the card room and wanted to see me when I returned. The game in the card room was stud poker, a somewhat friendly version my father financed for the entertainment of the sporting crowd that frequented his establishment. I was often allowed to ferry libations and sustenance to the players as a means of supplementing my allowance.

Dad peered through the haze of tobacco smoke. "Did you meet the champ?"

"And Rocca too!" I beamed.

The characters around the table all had comments about Joe Louis and what a shame it was that he'd been reduced to "rasslin."

"Did you get his autograph?" one asked.

"Yeah," I answered, "he signed a program for me, but the ref took it to give back to the promoter because I didn't pay for the program."

"Deal me out," Dad said, and we went to the hotel dining room. The waiter brought us apple pie, with milk for me and coffee for my father. Dad asked for the details of my adventure, and I told all, including the confiscation of my Joe Louis autograph.

Two days passed, and I was called to the hotel bar, where my dad and the wrestling referee were perched on stools. As I approached, the ref got to his feet and handed me the program with "Good Luck Kid—Joe Louis" scrawled on its face. The promoter said, "You should have this, Kip."

Two weeks later, I was dating Dawn, the ref's daughter. Although closely chaperoned by her mother, we managed some hand-holding at the movies and a little smooching in the backseat of her father's car on the ride home. A couple of family dinners at their home never led to anything serious, and after all these years, I remain curious as to how I hooked up with the girl (Could it be? No way!).

Life's journey would lead me to Joe Louis again, some 2,500 miles away and twenty years later, during a trip to Las Vegas. The champ was working as a greeter at a Vegas Strip hotel, glad-handing high rollers and celebs, posing for pictures, and signing autographs. He seemed bigger now; his face lit up with a genuine smile, and his eyes were bright with mirth. The hotel management provided two cornermen to keep the line of guests moving, the hellos quick, and the small talk brief.

I chose not to join the rest of the people in my party for photos with the champ. I was happy just watching, knowing things were going pretty good for both Joe and this "Good Luck Kid."

## Knockout Chili

Ingredients:
4 slices bacon
1 pound ground beef
1 pound ground pork
2 large onions, peeled and diced
3 cloves garlic, peeled and minced
1 large bell pepper, seeded and diced
2 jalapeños, seeded and diced
4 tablespoons dark red chili powder
1 tablespoon ground cumin
1 tablespoon salt
1/2 teaspoon pepper
1 (14-ounce) can diced tomatoes

1 (14-ounce) can crushed tomatoes
1 (15-ounce) can red chili beans, drained
1 (15-ounce) can pinto beans, drained
2 tablespoons dark brown sugar (optional)

Brown the bacon in a large stockpot until crisp. Remove bacon and cool. Crumble.

Add beef and pork to drippings and brown. Return crumbled bacon bits to meat, and add onion, garlic, bell pepper, jalapeños, chili powder, cumin, salt, and pepper. Cook and stir until incorporated into meat mixture.

Add remaining ingredients. Cook covered on low heat for 2 hours, stirring occasionally. Remove lid and simmer for a while longer if too thin.

### Pico de Gallo

I like to top a bowl with a spoonful of Pico de Gallo, but the champ liked his chili plain.

Ingredients:
4 roma tomatoes, diced
1 medium Spanish onion, peeled and diced
2 jalapeños, seeded and finely diced
1/2 cup chopped fresh cilantro leaves

juice of 2 limes
1/2 teaspoon kosher salt

Combine ingredients in a bowl. Cover and refrigerate 2 hours. Mix again before serving.

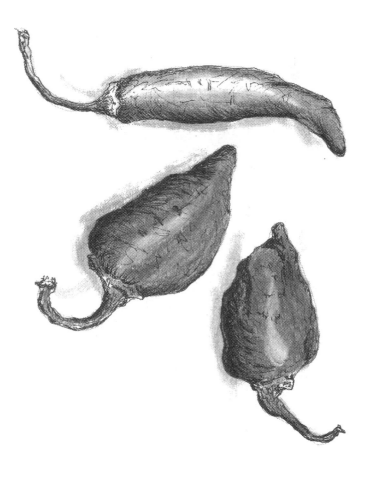

Adding spice to my life

## Sour Cream Corn Bread

Corn bread goes great with chili. A box and a half of Jiffy corn bread mix can be substituted for the dry ingredients in the following recipe. The results will be a little sweeter.

Ingredients:
1 1/2 cups yellow cornmeal
1 cup all-purpose flour
1 1/2 tablespoons baking powder
1 teaspoon baking soda
1 teaspoon salt
2 eggs, beaten
1 cup sour cream
1 cup cream corn
2 tablespoons butter, melted, or bacon drippings
2 tablespoons honey

Preheat oven to 400 degrees F.

Combine dry ingredients in a large mixing bowl. In another bowl whisk together the wet ingredients.

Pour wet ingredients into dry and mix with a spoon. Don't over mix.

Pour batter into a greased 9 × 2–inch cast iron skillet. Bake 25–30 minutes, or until knife inserted into center comes out clean.

# Chapter 12

## *Ginny Stines*

Ginny Stines was a petite dynamo with hair like a corn broom and a laugh as refreshing as ice-cold lemonade on a July afternoon. Her appetite for life was that of a gourmand. She was the wife of my best friend, a retired New York City detective named Dick. Being raised in the Little Italy section of the city developed her enthusiasm for the culinary arts, leading to a life as a restaurateur, with eateries in New York, Los Angeles, and Connecticut. She also delved into catering for Hollywood studios, weddings, and other events, but she was at her best when creating dinners for family and friends.

I met Ginny and Dick at a Los Angeles Little League organizing meeting in February 1970. Dick came up to me after I finished addressing the group and introduced himself by saying, "Hey, you talk like us!" An exchange of pleasantries revealed everything we had in common besides a New York accent. Our families soon became intertwined through our love of Little League baseball, police work, and Italian food. Our bond would last into the next century.

Some twenty-five years later, during my association with the Ogle Haus Inn, a pearl nestled on the banks of the Ohio River, Ginny and Dick visited us from their home in San Francisco. They marveled at the old-world feel of the hotel, the quaint shops of Vevay's downtown, and the beauty of an early summer on the Ohio. After a few days of cajoling, I got Ginny into the Ogle Haus kitchen to make her signature marinara sauce.

The kitchen staff gathered round and provided sous-chef assistance as Ginny did her cooking show. The ohs and ahs were not as much about the demonstrated techniques as her diamond-encrusted gold jewelry being flecked with tomato sauce.

Soon the aromatics of onion, garlic, herbs, and spices simmering with tomatoes in olive oil had us all salivating. The choice of wine for the sauce proved daunting, since the hotel's wine cellar lacked a robust Chianti. We settled for a French

Burgundy with a hefty pedigree. The director of the charitable foundation that controlled the hotel never forgave me for using the very last bottle of his favorite vintage.

"Never cook with cheap wine," Ginny explained as she poured a generous amount. The remaining two glasses were sipped as the marinara mellowed on a low flame.

As I looked forward to a dinner rarely served at the inn, I made a mental note to compliment the director for his fine taste in wines.

Ginny's heart of gold more than matched her 14K jewelry; her spirit out-sparkled her many diamonds. Sadly, my friends are no longer with us, their full and happy lives having ended a few years back. I'm sure Ginny would be happy for me to share her recipe with my readers. Just remember to wear some jewels and drink some wine while stirring Ginny's marinara sauce.

## Ginny's Marinara

Ingredients:
1/2 cup extra-virgin olive oil
1/2 stick butter
1 large sweet onion, finely chopped
4 large cloves garlic, peeled and pressed
1 (6-ounce) can tomato paste
1 large carrot, cut lengthwise
1 (28-ounce) can peeled plum tomatoes
1 (15-ounce) can tomato sauce
1/4 cup packed fresh basil, chopped

1/4 cup packed fresh Italian parsley, chopped
1 teaspoon sea salt
1/2 teaspoon fresh ground pepper
1/4 teaspoon dried rosemary
1/4 teaspoon dried oregano
2 cups premium red wine

Heat oil and butter in a heavy 4-quart saucepan. Sauté onion until soft and clear, about 4 minutes. Don't brown onion. Add garlic and continue cooking 1 minute. Add tomato paste. Stir and cook 4–5 minutes. Add carrot.

Mash plum tomatoes in your hand and add to pan with all the juice. Let simmer about 10 minutes, stirring frequently.

Add tomato sauce, basil, parsley, salt, pepper, rosemary, and oregano. Simmer about 15 minutes.

Add wine and simmer over low heat about 30 minutes, stirring frequently. When volume is reduced by half the sauce is ready.

Serve over your favorite pasta with an antipasto plate, garlic bread, and Parmesan cheese.

This is the base sauce for a great shrimp scampi. Just add a tablespoon each of red pepper flakes and lemon zest and the juice from one lemon to the sauce. Add a pound of uncooked shrimp, simmer for 10 minutes and serve over linguine cooked al dente.

Note: The carrot in this recipe is used as a flavoring. I usually eat it before serving the sauce. Sometimes Ginny would substitute a stalk or two of fresh fennel for the carrot to see if Dick was paying attention.

# Chapter 13

## *The Duke*

Our patrol car was cruising Ventura Boulevard when the "all units" call came out.

"Four fifty-nine. Burglar there now. Ten adam ninety-one, code two!"

I rogered the call while my partner negotiated a U-turn and hit the gas. Thirty seconds later, radio dispatch advised of a second call.

"See the cab driver. Male mental. Same location."

I acknowledged the additional information, and we turned off the boulevard into Encino Hills. Two blocks later, we pulled behind the Hollywood cab and its agitated driver. He quickly told us he had picked up his fare on Sunset and that during the thirty-minute drive to where we stood, he got creeped out by his passenger. Upon arrival at their destination, the fare told the cabbie to wait, got out of the vehicle, and jumped the six-foot wall surrounding the estate. So we rang the bell, and the large carved wooden gate swung open.

The first thing I noticed about John Wayne was his gun—it was bigger than mine. He held his hog leg down at his side and waved his "follow me, men" command. Whether behind a *Stagecoach*, crossing the *Rio Bravo*, or heading to his ranch on the *Red River*, we would have followed John Wayne anywhere, even though his pajamas and slippers seemed like a mistake of the studio's wardrobe department.

He told us that he had retired for the evening when aroused from his sleep by the screams of his housekeeper. She had responded to a knock on the door, and a young man had tried to force his way in. She blocked his effort with her considerable girth and punched him in the nose, dropping the intruder down the front steps.

Convinced the trespasser was still on the grounds, we searched the stables, garages, and guest cottage. This led us to the main house. I opened an outside cellar door and found the culprit half hidden under a small tarp. I dragged him out and asked Wayne if he knew the arrestee.

"I never saw this SOB in my life!" he said. He then proceeded to ask the guy why he had come to his home.

"I needed to talk to you, Mr. Wayne," the man sobbed, blood trickling from his nose. "I took a cab to get here and don't have the money to pay the driver."

As we finished up at the scene and got John Wayne to autograph the crime complaint, the cabbie walked up the quarter-mile driveway to ask who was paying the fare. Wayne handed him a big bill and sent him on his merry way.

Leaning into the window of our cruiser, Wayne told our shackled prisoner, "I took care of the cab, but you're on the hook for the rest of this."

After booking our prisoner, my partner and I had a craving for rare steak, pinto beans, and black coffee. Absent a chuck wagon, we settled for chiliburgers and cheese fries at an outdoor stand on the boulevard and contemplated the stars of the Hollywood sky.

You don't have to go west of the Pecos to cowboy up for a meal prepared on an open fire. (If you don't want to camp out, you can do this on your stove top, but it seems to taste better on a wood fire.) You'll need a large cast iron frying pan to do this right.

## Cowboy Steak and Pinto Beans

Ingredients:
2 slices bacon
1 thick-sliced rib eye steak, 1 1/4 pounds or more
salt and pepper to taste
2 tablespoons Dijon mustard
2 tablespoons minced onion
2 tablespoons Worcestershire sauce
1 (15-ounce) can pinto beans

Place pan on fire and let it heat up. Fry the bacon, and remove from pan.

Salt and pepper steak on both sides, and then smear one side with half the mustard.

Add onion to bacon drippings and place steak in pan, mustard side down. While one side is searing, pour the Worcestershire on the steak and spread with remaining mustard.

Flip steak after about 4 minutes, and cook second side for an additional 4 minutes. Remove to warm platter to rest.

Add beans and reserved cooked bacon slices to the frying pan and thoroughly heat, stirring to incorporate all the pan drippings and break up the bacon. I like to mash some of the beans to thicken up the mixture.

Slice the steak across the grain into 1/4-inch slices and serve with the beans.

A salad would be nice, along with a pot of chicory-laced coffee to wash it all down. The Duke liked his black.

*Note: Some years later, another of life's quirks would find me a guest of the Duke's son, Patrick Wayne, in his dugout box at Dodger Stadium for a Dodgers-Giants game.*

# Chef's Notes:

_____

_____

_____

_____

_____

_____

_____

_____

_____

_____

_____

_____

_____

_____

_____

_____

_____

_____

_____

_____

# Chapter 14

## *Captain Santa*

There are many ways to measure a man. There is a Shakespeare line—"the evil that men do lives after them while the good is oft interred with their bones"—that certainly speaks of the infamy of villainy. That may be true, but let me tell a story with a different point of view.

I've been thinking of one holiday season and a friend of mine, the late Bob Tucker. When measured by the good in his heart, by how he reacted to adversity, and by how he behaved when he believed no one was watching, Bob was a very good man.

Bob was a captain of the Los Angeles Police Department and a captain in the US Navy. He drank like a sailor and cursed like one too, but these were more virtues than faults. Most who worked for Bob were fiercely loyal because he was loyal to them. He took an interest in our successes and failures when our efforts were sincere but was stern to those who didn't give their best.

Christmas was not an easy time for my captain, not since one of his men's brothers, also an officer, was shot execution-style while most of us were attending our divisional Christmas party.

Word came to us right after dinner. The news ripped through the gathering, and we quickly dispersed. We were over twenty miles from the scene of the crime. All of us wanted to do something, but of course we couldn't. Bob, as commanding officer, did what he could to console the fallen officer's family and meet their needs during the weeks that followed.

Time marches on. Two years later, another Christmas was approaching.

In the late sixties a man I will call Jacob escaped from Eastern European communism, taking his father and sister with him. Eventually they made their way to Los Angeles, and Jacob found a position with the LAPD. He was our station house janitor. He did his job with a cheerful vigor that we sworn personnel truly admired.

One Thanksgiving, he was told he had an illness that would soon take his life. He worked at the station for a few more weeks with a sadness about him that all could see. When he was put on medical leave, he knew he would not return. A fund was set up, the rank and file all pitching in. Most gave what they could, some gave even more. It helped that Christmas was but a few days away.

On December 21, 1975, Bob Tucker donned a Santa Claus outfit, beard, wig, and all. We loaded "Santa" into a patrol car, along with all the fixings for a fine Christmas dinner, and drove to Jacob's home.

The fund raised a little over $1,000—big bucks back then. I saw a tear in Santa's eye when he handed the family a check for $1,500. One of the officers said to me, "I didn't know we raised that much."

"We didn't," I said, pointing to our captain. "We're only Santa's Helpers!"

On Christmas Day, Jacob's sister showed up at the police station with a tray of stuffed cabbage rolls she had prepared for the troops. Jacob and his father stayed outside in the car.

"Merry Christmas," she said, placing the tray on the front counter. A stash of paper plates and plastic forks soon appeared, and the aroma of her cabbage rolls soon drew a crowd of officers from throughout the station.

I received this recipe from Jacob's sister a few days after Christmas. Sadly, Jacob passed away the following February.

## Stuffed Cabbage Rolls

Ingredients:
1 head cabbage
1 pound lean ground beef
salt and pepper to taste
1 medium onion, diced
1 cup instant rice
zest and juice of 1 lemon
1 (15-ounce) can diced tomatoes, undrained
1 (8-ounce) can tomato sauce
1/2 cup packed brown sugar

Preheat oven to 350 degrees F.

Plunge head of cabbage into a large pot of boiling water. Remove pot from heat and let stand until head is cool enough to handle.

Separate wilted leaves, using the outer ones to line a 9 × 12–inch baking dish.

In large skillet, lightly cook the ground beef. Season beef with salt and pepper and add onion. Cook until onion is slightly wilted.

Add rice, lemon zest, and lemon juice to meat, mixing well. Remove from heat and let cool.

Wrap a heaping tablespoon of ground-beef mixture in individual cabbage leaf. Roll and place in lined baking dish, seam side down. Repeat until all meat is used.

Pour diced tomatoes evenly over top of cabbage rolls.

Combine tomato sauce and brown sugar. Spread evenly over all.

Bake 40 minutes.

These can be done in a Crock-Pot set on high heat for 2 hours, but they will require an additional 20 minutes to cook off some of the liquid after removing the top.

# Chef's Notes:

"Anyone got a match?"

It's a small world after all!

# Part 3

# *Places*

# Chapter 15

## *Growing Up with Seafood*

The vast majority of today's youth disdain seafood. I firmly believe they come by this through selective feeding. Canned tuna and frozen fish sticks  were not conceived to nurture a love for fish and other things from the sea. Let me explain.

I spent most of my life on one coast or the other and developed a love for our great oceans as a young man. Some of my fondest memories are of fishing the surf at Montauk, the bays of Catalina, and the blue of the Sea of Cortez; of clamming in South Shore and at Pismo; of crabbing the Chesapeake; and of shrimping in the Florida Keys. I could fill a book with these adventures, and perhaps someday I will. But these experiences pale in comparison to the memory of when my dad took me fishing on the Isle of Manhattan!

The early fifties were a great time to be a kid. Saturday morning television had yet to capture the hearts and minds of America's youth. My dad had just parlayed his taxi business into a hotel, where we lived in a three-room suite on the second floor. My Saturday mornings consisted of working in and around the hotel while most of my contemporaries had more idyllic pursuits.

Dad's business style was hands-on, and he involved himself in every aspect of the operation, including making sure I had enough chores to keep me off the streets and away from the activities of my hoodlum buddies, as he liked to refer to my friends. Any protestations on my part could well trigger Dad's hands-on management style. Thus I became a willing participant in the education of Kip.

One Friday in the summer of 1955, my dad informed me that he and I were going fishing in the morning and that I should be ready to go at five o'clock. I was so excited that I couldn't get to sleep until well past midnight. He woke me at four and told me to meet him in the hotel kitchen in twenty minutes. There we breakfasted on sweet rolls and coffee prepared by Chef Wu, who, it turned out, was going on the trip with us. We set out on time and were crossing the Brooklyn Bridge before dawn.

The Manhattan skyline is a beautiful sight just before first light. We came off the bridge onto South Street and turned again onto Fulton, and there stood the famous Fulton Fish Market in all its glory.

There were bushels of clams and oysters, crates of fish of all types and sizes, and mountains of ice. Water tanks filled with live crabs and lobsters were everywhere. Squid and octopuses stared at me from a sea of crushed ice. I'll never forget the cacophony of fishmongers hawking their wares, the hustle and bustle of handcarts, pushcarts, forklifts, trucks, horns honking, bells ringing, whistles, and shouts. What excitement. What fishing!

We were back at the hotel before seven in the morning with enough seafood to feed the two hundred people expected at the first annual clambake the hotel was putting on that afternoon. And yes, I did my assigned chores before noon. Fishing builds character and an appetite.

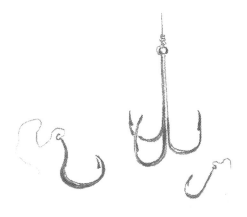

Get hooked!

## Halibut Steak with Orange and Ginger Shrimp Sauce

Ingredients:

*Steaks*
4 halibut steaks, 4–6 ounces each
1/4 cup soy sauce
4 teaspoons sesame oil

*Shrimp Sauce*
4 tablespoons butter
2 green onions, chopped
1 (8-ounce) can mandarin oranges, drained, liquid reserved
4 ounces salad shrimp

1 teaspoon freshly grated ginger
1/2 teaspoon minced garlic
1 tablespoon cornstarch

## For the Steaks

Rinse fish under cold water. Pat dry. Preheat grill or broiler.

Mix soy sauce and sesame oil and brush on fish.

Place fish on grill or in broiler and cook about 4 minutes, basting with soy mixture. Turn and repeat. Turn one more time. Baste and cook until desired doneness.

## For the Shrimp Sauce

Heat a one quart sauce pan and melt butter. Add onion and sauté 2 minutes on medium heat. Add shrimp, orange segments, ginger, and garlic, and continue to heat for about 4 minutes.

Mix cornstarch with four tablespoons of juice from the oranges, and then slowly stir into the shrimp mixture. Simmer on high heat for about 2 minutes to let sauce thicken. Set aside.

## To Assemble

Place each steak on a warmed plate. Top with shrimp sauce and serve with steamed rice and snow peas. Sake is optional, but I prefer a cold Japanese beer!

You can substitute shark, salmon, or swordfish steaks, but I favor Pacific halibut.

# Apple Cabbage Slaw

This slaw is a great salad to serve with this fish dish.

Ingredients:
4 cups chopped green cabbage
2 Granny Smith apples, cored and chopped
2 green onions, finely chopped
1/2 cup mayonnaise
1/4 cup apple cider vinegar
4 tablespoons sugar
1 teaspoon salt
1/2 teaspoon fresh ground black pepper

Mix all ingredients well. Refrigerate 2 hours before serving.

# Chapter 16

## *Monterey*

California's Monterey Peninsula is one of the most beautiful places in all America. It is famed for its Pebble Beach golf courses, the Monterey Bay Aquarium, and the scenic vistas of 17-Mile Drive. That I had the privilege to live there for a year and have since been able to revisit one of the best years of my life a dozen times or so makes it very special to me. And this all came about because of a birthday gift.

In the early 1950s, my grandmother Grace introduced me to the work of John Steinbeck. When she gave me the book, it would set the course of my life, make me a voracious reader of all things Steinbeck, and ultimately influence my choice of reading, writing, and fishing as avocations.

In his book *Cannery Row,* Steinbeck weaves a tale of place and characters whose flaws and virtues are celebrated in descriptive prose laced with vivid metaphors. I was hooked, and when Uncle Sam offered me the opportunity to live in Monterey for all of 1959, I jumped at the chance.

A second-story apartment on a Monterey hillside provided an unobstructed view of the bay and the legendary Cannery Row, all for seventy-five dollars a month. A year of schooling at the Presidio of Monterey provided the added bonus of walking the alleys and streets of Steinbeck's prose. I experienced the smells of the canneries, strolled the beaches, explored the tidal pools, and fished the shores. It was easy to imagine rubbing shoulders with his characters. I witnessed the cultural diversity of which he wrote, which was reflected in the many languages spoken and the different ethnic cuisines served in the area's many eateries.

Within the year, I learned to speak, read, and write another language. I also read most of Steinbeck's novels. His writing changed the way I looked at people. I became an ardent people-watcher and developed an ability to read people, a skill that served me well during my two stints in the military, my two decades in law enforcement, and the time in which I've owned a number of businesses, employing many hundreds.

One Saturday in the summer of 1959, a number of us students charted a fishing boat for a half-day excursion. I had a lot of deep-sea fishing experience, growing up never more than twenty minutes from the Atlantic. My companions this day were neophytes, but they were eager to test their sea legs. We pushed off from the dock a little past one o'clock for an afternoon of cod fishing in the three-hundred-foot-deep water some four miles out. The bay was made choppy by an onshore breeze that the forty-foot vessel's six-hundred horses easily handled.

Once we were at the skipper's favorite spot, the mate handed out stubby deep-sea poles equipped with railing plates and multigeared reels strung with eighty-pound test. A five-foot leader held four hooks and a three-pound weight to the end of the line. Next the mate instructed the novices in baiting the hooks and getting the rig to the bottom.

Ocean swells travel great distances, pushed and steered by weather and current. This day, six-foot swells forced the skipper to take them head on, thus creating a gentle rocking motion that moved our weighted lines up and down. The moving bait proved irresistible to the cod, and soon we were reeling them in three or four at a time.

Deepwater fish aren't built for atmospheric pressure of 14.5 psi, which is about one hundredth of the pressure the fish just came from, so they kind of explode a bit. Getting the hook out of a fish with bulged eyes and a protruding bladder that is regurgitating the bait is an arduous task for the uninitiated. The increasing size and frequency of the swells didn't help. Soon over half our party started chumming over the side.

An hour in, the swells had reached rail high, and only four of us remained on deck reeling in the fish. Finally, the skipper announced, "Time to call it a day, boys. The hands will gladly clean your catch for a generous tip."

Seasick green is not a pleasant color, nor was the grey of the clouds closing in from the west as we headed to port. Gulls raucously dove in our wake for scraps of the fish cleaning, which were being thrown from the aft of the boat. It was a great afternoon of fishing—at least for some of us.

To top it off, I won the pool for biggest fish; it was a three-foot Ling cod big enough to feed a family of ten. Of course, as in any good fishing story, you should have seen the one that got away!

Cod is a mild-tasting fish whose filets are a chef favorite. But for how long? I wonder if any fishery can withstand the demands of an exploding human population and the continued pollution of our seas. For now, Pacific and Atlantic cod are available, though not as readily as only a generation ago. Because of dwindling stocks and mandated quota reductions, many of America's cod fishermen have gone out of business. Enjoy 'em while you can.

## Cod Filets with Olive and Bacon Sauce

Ingredients:
1 tablespoon canola oil
2 tablespoons butter
1/4 cup flour
salt and pepper to taste
2 (6-ounce) cod filets
2 tablespoons cooked bacon crumbles
1 tablespoon drained capers
2 tablespoons chopped kalamata olives
2 ounces white wine

juice of half a lemon
3 ounces heavy cream
1 teaspoon chopped fresh parsley

Heat oil over medium-high heat and add butter.

Season flour with salt and pepper. Dredge filets in seasoned flour and sauté until golden brown, 3–4 minutes per side. Remove filets to dish. Cover and keep warm.

Turn heat to high and add bacon, capers, and olives. Mix while cooking 3 minutes.

Deglaze pan with wine and lemon juice. Simmer to reduce liquid by half. Stir in cream and parsley. Remove from heat.

Place cod filet on pile of steamed rice. Spoon sauce onto fish and drizzle plate. A lemon wedge and a tomato rosette on a lettuce leaf will complete the presentation nicely.

# Chapter 17

## *Different "Italian"*

Italian food enjoys a universal popularity in its many different forms. Pasta, a basic Italian fare, has its roots in China. A recent archeological find of a bowl of noodles dating back to around 2000 BC established that the Chinese were eating pasta long before the Italians. Many believe that Marco Polo introduced pasta to the Italian peninsula, where it became an art form. Surely he had no idea what he was starting! The Italians created hundreds of variations of the basic noodle and thousands of ways to fix them.

When I travel, I like to try the local Italian food and have been pleasantly surprised in such diverse locations as Seoul, Korea; Tokyo, Japan; and Mazatlán, Mexico. While visiting Tokyo in the early 1960s, I wandered a few blocks off the Ginza and stumbled on a little place called Nicola's. I followed the unmistakable scent of roasted garlic and simmering tomato sauce. Upon entering, I was struck by the eclectic mix of a New York Italian having kimono-clad waitresses serving shoeless patrons sitting on the floor around an eight-inch-high table, eating pizza and drinking Sapporo beer.

Nick was an ex-GI who never left Japan after the war. His real name was Alphonso, but Nick was easier to say for Japanese speakers. His story was unique, and the food was good, though somewhat modified to suit his customer base. He had some unusual pizza toppings, including squid and sea urchin. I enjoyed a pasta dish with fried octopus and a sauce darkened with squid ink!

In Seoul, I learned to eat spaghetti with chop sticks. Korean Italian is very hot and very spicy. All meals are accompanied by a bowl of raw, peeled garlic cloves and a dish of hot pepper sauce made for dipping. The restaurant I went to was named Italy Noodle. The chef, who spoke no English or Italian, was hoping to obtain some Italian cheeses before the 1988 Seoul Olympics. I put him in contact with a Korean friend of mine in Los Angeles who worked diligently to meet his needs at the highest bearable price.

In Mexico, I discovered linguine tossed with roasted chili peppers, butter, and goat cheese. The chef was from Milan, spoke reasonable English, and was in dire need of some decent Italian wines. On my next trip to Mazatlán, I smuggled in four bottles of Chianti and a bottle of Anisette liqueur. Milo was so happy that he barbecued a goat, and we feasted for hours. I often wonder if this goat was the source of the cheese I ate on my first visit to Milo's.

## Milo's Linguine with Roasted Peppers and Goat Cheese

Roasting peppers makes them explode with flavor and allows you to remove the skin for easier digestion.

Ingredients:
1 red bell pepper
1 green bell pepper
2 tablespoons butter
2 tablespoons flour
1 cup milk
8 ounces goat's-milk fontina cheese, shredded

salt and pepper
2 cloves garlic, peeled and minced
2 tablespoons olive oil
1 pound linguine pasta, cooked al dente

Stick a fork in stem end of both peppers and hold them directly over a flame to char, turning to get all sides.

Place charred peppers in a paper bag and seal. Allow peppers to cool for a few minutes and then remove to peel. Skin will slide right off under running tap water.

Halve and seed peeled peppers, and then cut into julienne strips. Set aside.

Melt butter in a medium saucepan. Stir in flour to make a roux. Don't let flour brown. Whisk in milk and let mixture simmer until it thickens.

Sprinkle cheese into sauce a little at a time, continuing to stir until cheese starts to melt. Salt and pepper to taste. Set aside.

In a large skillet, heat olive oil and sauté garlic. Don't let garlic brown. Add julienned peppers and toss to heat thoroughly. Add cheese sauce and cooked linguine, tossing to mix all the ingredients.

Serve with crusty bread and a robust Chianti. Milo loves you!

# Chef's Notes:

_____

_____

_____

_____

_____

_____

_____

_____

_____

_____

_____

_____

_____

_____

_____

_____

_____

_____

_____

_____

# Chapter 18

## *Mountain Men*

The Thanksgiving weekend of '63 helped put the holiday in perspective for me. A couple of friends and I planned a hunting trip to Mount Shasta, a five-hundred-mile trek from the Los Angeles suburbs. Accommodations were arranged by a relative of one of my hunting buddies.

Loaded for bear, we arrived at dusk just as snow began falling. We left 70-degree temperatures in LA, but as we unloaded our gear, the temperature was well below freezing. Over a supper of warm chili and corn bread, washed down by a couple of cold ones, our host outlined our planned hunt, which was scheduled to begin an hour before sunup. Anticipation of an adventure long in the planning made sleep difficult, and soon our wake-up call got us in motion.

Stepping from our cabin, we were introduced by our host to our guides and hunting companions. Surely the inspiration for the *Deliverance* movie stood before us, along with six hounds prancing through a foot of overnight snow. The predawn temperature was in the teens. Our vehicles were a four-wheel-drive pickup and a WWII Jeep two-seater with gun racks and a wooden game box the size of a small coffin. We were told by our guides that grizzlies were no longer on the mountain and that they had been replaced by a lot of black bears. Cougars had been recently sighted; they were out of season but could be shot to save the dogs.

As I huddled in the back of the pickup with four of the dogs for warmth, I wondered if these animals were ever bathed. We drove to the town dump and set the hounds loose. They soon hit the scent of a foraging bear, and the barking chase was on. I joined our two guides on the Jeep, glad to be armed with rifle and sidearm. As we rode toward the baying hounds, sunlight broke on the mountain. We followed the noise of the pack by traversing old logging trails for over an hour, waiting for the barking to change to howls, signaling the treeing of the bear.

The treeing led to a half-hour hike into a heavily wooded draw. We were met by a wounded dog and his five howling partners at the base of a forty-foot tree with a bear on top. Our host asked if we wanted the shot. Proudly, none of us saw the sport in it, and we declined. The owner of the wounded dog exacted his revenge, and we helped pull the dogs from the fallen bear. On the cold ride back to the cabin that Thanksgiving Day of 1963, with the clawed dog on my lap, I resolved never to hunt animals again.

The following dish goes good with bear steak, but it is even better with turkey or ham. You can make your own variation by adding a favorite spice or herb or a substitute cheese.

## Buttered Squash Casserole

Ingredients:
1/4 pound butter
1 medium onion, thinly sliced
2 pounds of your favorite squash, washed, seeded and cut into 1/2-inch cubes
1 red bell pepper, washed, seeded, and julienned
1 clove garlic, minced
salt and pepper to taste
1 cup shredded cheddar cheese
1 cup bread crumbs

Preheat oven to 350 degrees F.

Sauté onion in butter until translucent.

Add garlic, peppers, and squash, and liberally season with salt and pepper. Stir and cover. Reduce heat, and continue cooking until squash begins to soften.

Place squash mixture into a buttered 2-quart casserole. Stir in cheese, and top with bread crumbs. Bake uncovered 20 minutes.

Remove and let stand for 10 minutes before serving. Voilà!

# Chapter 19

## *Up, Up, and Away*

Up, up, and away! No, it's not Superman; it's me entering the Fifth Dimension in my beautiful balloon with my honey by my side. As we float some two hundred feet above the suburban Louisville countryside, I marvel at how far hot air has taken me.

We're in the Coca-Cola balloon, piloted by Jimmy Litsey, and we are joined by seven other colorful hot air balloons on a perfect Sunday evening of clear skies and balmy air. Our enthusiastic captain, a proud member of a small fraternity of skilled breeze riders, eases us down to treetop level, seeking nuances of a shifting breeze. Then we gently ascend to five hundred feet with a few blasts from his gas burner, which supplies more hot air to the nylon bag that billows for a hundred feet above our heads.

The popularity of hot air ballooning today was made possible by a concept developed by a man named Ed Yost back in 1960. An aeronautical engineer, he came up with the idea of burning bottled propane gas to fill a nylon envelope with hot air to generate lift. His jury-rigged prototype involving a couple of aluminum lawn chairs got him a twenty-five-minute inaugural flight. He went on to establish the balloonist fraternity and set many world records in the process. The state of New Mexico honors Ed Yost with a depiction of a hot air balloon on its license plates.

Dogs bark, kids wave, and people interrupt their backyard barbecues to shout hellos as we float gently by. A ground crew of three races the countryside in a chase car tethered to our wicker basket by radio. Jimmy points them out as our shadow crosses the Gene Snyder Freeway. Downtown Louisville looms on the horizon while we pass over Gentry Estates, dotted with horses, ponds, and corrals. Other balloonists follow Jimmy's lead as he searches for a safe landing zone accessible to the chasers. He selects a hillock in a fishing park and radios his intent. We watch the venting of air that allows the ground to come up to greet us. Jimmy's instructions prepare us for a hard landing that never materializes, and the ground crew catches us like Willie Mays closing in on a can of corn.

Champagne toasts celebrate a wonderful adventure. Other balloons and crews dot the landing area, and Jimmy checks the well-being of all before our chase-car ride back to where we began some two hours earlier.

If only a wicker picnic basket awaited, maybe containing a twilight repast of cold lemon chicken and an Italian-style potato salad to be washed down by a frosty beverage. This would surely complete the perfect day. Too bad the reality of a ninety-minute drive has us scurrying to our car. Instead, we catch a bite at one of the many fast-food joints along the way, hoping our hungry cats at home appreciate our sacrifice. Perhaps another time ...

## Picnic-Basket Chicken

Ingredients:
1 (2-1/2 to 3-pound) fryer chicken, cut into pieces
1/2 cup fresh mint leaves
1/4 cup extra-virgin olive oil
4 cloves garlic, peeled and pressed

1 tablespoon sugar
juice of two lemons
1 teaspoon lemon zest
1/2 teaspoon salt
1/2 teaspoon pepper

Wash chicken under running water, and pat dry with paper towel. Place in large bowl.

Place remaining ingredients in blender, and pulse blend until frothy. Pour over chicken, and cover. Marinate in refrigerator for at least 4 hours or overnight.

Remove from marinade, and grill, roast, or bake chicken until done. Each cooking method adds its own subtleties to the flavor profile.

### Italian Potato Salad

Ingredients:
2 pounds red-skinned potatoes, halved and then cut into 1/4-inch-thick slices
3 quarts water
3 tablespoons salt
1 (14-ounce) can Italian green beans, drained
1 medium red onion, peeled and thinly sliced

1 pint cherry tomatoes, halved
1 cup of your favorite Italian dressing

Boil potato slices in salted water until al dente. Rinse in cold tap water to cool. Drain.

Toss in large bowl with rest of ingredients. Cover and refrigerate at least 2 hours.

This meal will travel well in your picnic basket. Serve with a chilled beverage. Maybe Asti Spumante? Enjoy the ride!

# Chef's Notes:

_____

_____

_____

_____

_____

_____

_____

_____

_____

_____

_____

_____

_____

_____

_____

_____

_____

_____

_____

_____

_____

# Chapter 20

## *Black Hills Gold*

We come out of Rapid City heading for adventure. Two towns of Western lore, Lead and Deadwood, wait to surprise and entertain. A waxing crescent moon lights our way into the Black Hills of South Dakota. We are in the land of General Custer, Wild Bill Hickok, and Calamity Jane. Knowing that Chief Crazy Horse, Bill Cody, and Wyatt Earp preceded us down this trail adds to our excitement.

A rustic saloon awaits our dinner dollars, and an hour's winding drive of ups and downs gets us there. Country-western music fills the crowded parking lot of Elk Creek Steak House and Saloon. I watch a couple of cowboys dismount their pickup truck, adjust their ten-gallon hats, and brush the dust from their boots on the back of their jeans. I do the same. Except for the neon beer signs and lighted parking lot, it is easy to imagine the vehicles being horses and carriages and that I've somehow traveled back to a time of more than a century ago.

We walk past hitching posts to the entrance alcove and are presented with two doors. The quieter one, marked "Diner," is our choice. Upon entering, we are greeted by a hearty "Hello" and are quickly seated amid a faux rodeo motif that gives us hope of sating our meat-and-potato appetites.

Our waitress presents us menus with the same cheery verve that greeted our arrival. The offerings of Angus beef, elk, and buffalo are balanced with walleye and trout. She answers all our questions knowledgably so no one would be disappointed with their choices. I've traveled a thousand miles for buffalo meat, and although the bison short ribs sound very tempting, I opt for the 12-ounce New York buffalo steak with a baked potato, preceded by a spinach salad. The others of our party play it safe with their choices, except Linda, who risks the potatoes au gratin to go with her petite prime rib, medium rare.

A nice wine list complimented the offerings, and this proved to be the best meal of our five-day visit. We all left happy, and if we ever get back to the Black Hills, we'll surely make the steakhouse in Elk Creek a must-stop. If you happen to get there before me, tell them Kip sent you.

I shared some of my buffalo steak with my three companions so they wouldn't ask "What does it taste like?" For those of you who don't know, the answer is, "It tastes like buffalo." Similar to beef, it takes on some of the characteristics of what the animal eats. Restaurants don't just go out and shoot a bison and cut it up in their kitchens. Meat is purchased from reliable suppliers, and many farms and ranches raise buffalo just like cattle. In fact, bison are being raised in Switzerland County, a few miles outside of Vevay.

A buffalo steak doesn't appreciate a lot of cooking. If you don't like your steak rare or medium rare, bring along your favorite Eskimo to prechew your medium to medium-well-done steak. Well-done buffalo is best worn on the soles of your feet.

The Elk Creek chefs limited themselves to just a little salt and pepper, allowing the full flavor of the meat, and only the meat, to tantalize the taste buds. If I was cooking the meat, I'd probably grill it on the hot coals of a hard wood, preferably hickory, and I would wait until the wood was burnt down enough to minimize the smoke. I would also recommend the steak be served on a heated platter, with nothing else on the plate to interfere with the meat's distinct flavor.

When the butcher is done cutting the strip steaks, porterhouses, and tenderloins, the rest is best ground up to make delightful burgers, which were featured in about half the restaurants we visited. We also were teased with buffalo chili and buffalo stew, and if left on my own, I'd have undoubtedly tried them all. But I did get away with a recipe for Buffalo Stew.

## Buffalo, Elk, or Venison Stew

Ingredients:
2 tablespoons butter
2 tablespoons canola oil
2 tablespoons rendered buffalo fat or bacon drippings
1 pound buffalo steak, cut into 1-inch cubes

1 teaspoon salt
1 teaspoon black pepper
1/2 teaspoon ground sage
1/2 teaspoon tarragon
1 cup biscuit mix, divided
4 large carrots, peeled and quartered
2 medium onions, peeled and quartered
2 bay leaves
4 medium potatoes, washed and halved
1 cup chopped celery, with leaves
1 (14-ounce) can chicken stock
1 (12-ounce) bottle of beer

In a heavy-bottomed 4-quart pot, heat oil and drippings on medium-high. Meanwhile, sprinkle salt, pepper, sage, and tarragon on meat. Dredge the cubes in half the biscuit mix.

Brown meat in the hot fat, stirring with wooden spoon. Add onion, carrots, and bay leaves along with half the chicken stock, deglazing bottom of pot by stirring with spoon.

When onion quarters start to separate, add potatoes and celery. Cover and reduce heat. Simmer 20 minutes.

In a small saucepan, make a roux with butter, remaining biscuit mix, and a little of the stock. When it gets smooth and creamy, remove from heat, cover, and set aside.

Add beer and rest of stock to stew and continue to simmer another 20 minutes.

Remove the bay leaves, if you wish, and stir in roux. Another 20 minutes of simmering should thicken it up quite nicely.

Before you put the biscuit mix back in the cupboard, make some biscuits to go with your buffalo stew.

# Chef's Notes:

# Chapter 21

## *Key Largo*

The last of the evening shower passed, taking the clouds with it. Though the air had cooled a bit, the humidity persisted. Looking west, you could see the gulf extinguishing the sun as we busily prepared our twelve-foot skiff. The dusk that allowed us to stow our gear had also brought hordes of mosquitoes to feed upon us. Perhaps the smell of beer and Cuban sandwiches stoked their bloodlust enough for them to penetrate the fog of insect repellant we sprayed upon ourselves.

Roger started up the ten-horse kicker on his first pull as I untied the bowline and pushed off from the dock. He put it in gear and fed it some gas. Soon we were headed across Largo Bay, a series of lighted channel markers guiding us to the cut in the mangroves. Looking upward, I marveled at a night's sky full of stars and a sliver of moon while the put-put of the little engine helped our skiff skim along at a modest seven knots.

It would be an hour before the ebbing tide would reverse its course. Roger wanted to be tied up to the mangrove tree that marked his favorite spot, where the incoming tide would bring us the bounty we sought. Once in place, we donned our miner's hats over mosquito netting and then doused ourselves with yet another round of repellant that did little to quiet the buzzing attacks. We turned on our helmet lights, floated a small spot on the water's surface, and awaited our prey as if on a snipe hunt.

Catching shrimp in the dark with flashlight and an eight-foot pole net is a sport for the hardy. Referred to as "bugs" by the locals, these shrimp prowl the mangroves for food, riding the tide in and out of the bays. They troll with their periscope eyes just above the surface, searching for some eats. We were doing pretty much the same, our lights reflecting off their tiny eyes, making easy targets for our nets. Well almost. Shrimp can jump, so Roger said you have to "be quick with your net." Who knew?

A good run lasts a couple of hours. And so, with our batteries low and a few hundred shrimp on board, Roger fired up the little engine, and we headed back to the dock, where I learned there was still work to be done.

Pinching the heads off two hundred live shrimp is an arduous task not to be undertaken by the fainthearted. In fact, the fainthearted shouldn't even watch.

"Look away," I admonished Linda, while I separated each head from its body. When done correctly, the gut comes away with the head in one operation. By the time I neared the end of our bucket, I was getting quite good at it. The heads and smaller shrimp were set aside for a gumbo base. The headless, unpeeled beauties, weighing out at sixteen to twenty per pound, were set aside for the next day's old-fashioned shrimp boil, tails and all.

I hear the shrimp don't run like they used to twenty-five years ago, but the mosquitoes still swarm the mangroves as ravenous as ever. Now, whenever I'm preparing shrimp, I think of those times spent with Linda in Key Largo when "we had it all, just like Bogie and Bacall."

# Shrimp Boil

Our species has been boiling stuff from the sea since way before cookbooks. Crab, lobster, and shrimp are mostly eaten boiled, although some guy from Australia was fond of putting his shrimp on a barbie. This recipe for a shrimp boil is very similar to a Cajun crawfish boil. The tradition of using corn on the cob and potatoes is an American one, dating back to Pilgrim times.

You need a heavy-bottomed stockpot, 8 quarts or larger, to make it correctly. Salt-free dieters need not apply; nor should those who lack timing. This will feed four to six with a loaf of crusty bread warm from the oven.

Ingredients:
6 quarts water
1 large lemon, halved
1 large onion, peeled and quartered
4 cloves garlic, peeled and mashed
1/4 cup Old Bay Seasoning
1/4 cup kosher salt
8 whole peppercorns
2 pounds small red potatoes, halved
4 ears corn, shucked and halved
2 pounds large shrimp, peeled, deveined

1/2 teaspoon cayenne pepper
hot sauce to taste

Bring water to a low boil and add next six
ingredients. Boil 5 minutes.

Add potatoes and boil 10 minutes.

Add corn and boil an additional 5 minutes.

Add shrimp, cayenne pepper, and hot sauce.
Cover pot and turn off heat. Wait 5 minutes. Drain
and serve.

A big bowl-like platter makes great presentation
center table. Pass the bread, please.

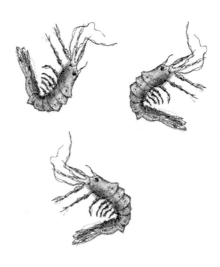

# Chapter 22

## *South of the Border*

The Sea of Cortez sits between the Baja Peninsula and the Mexican mainland. It is the site of one the best sport fisheries in the world. After six months of planning, our group of eight was on our way aboard a Mexicana flight from LAX to Cabo San Lucas. Shortly after crossing into Mexican airspace, we made an unscheduled landing at Mexicali airport. We assumed we were stopping for more cerveza, as our group had started to party hearty in the passenger lounge long before takeoff. Our jubilation came to an end when we looked out the windows to see three jeeploads of heavily armed *federales* surround our plane as it stopped at the end of the runway.

The pilot announced, first in Spanish and then in English, "Ladies and Gentlemen, please remain seated while the federal police board our plane to inspect your travel documents." A wheeled staircase allowed the six officers to come on board. The one in charge had as much scrambled egg on his hat as I had for breakfast. After a brief conversation with our pilot, he directed four of his officers down the aisle to the rear of the plane.

After inspecting the passenger manifest, he took the microphone and called, "Enrique Fuentes! Morales! Levantate!" But no one stood up.

The soldiers worked their way up from the rear of the plane, checking IDs as the man in charge watched. Suddenly, a man two rows in front of me made a break for the door. A quick beatdown had him quickly subdued. The woman in the window seat next to where the man, Enrique, had been sitting screamed, and she was also taken into custody.

Our craft was towed to a hanger, and we were directed to disembark with all our carry-on belongings. Mexican customs agents inspected our stuff while airline personnel unloaded all the checked luggage and set it on the tarmac outside the hanger. Each passenger was then required to claim his or her luggage. This process allowed the recovery of all Enrique's and his companion's property. This three-hour ordeal caused us to arrive in Cabo four hours late, long after the complimentary peanuts and beers ran out.

The next day's fishing was great, and the skipper had us back to our hotel by cocktail hour. A tequila tasting was accompanied by mariachis. When the tequilas all started tasting the same, we retired to our rooms. After showers and after-sun lotion had us all feeling human again, dinner was waiting on the hotel veranda.

Ceviche cocktails of the sea bass we plucked from the ocean but four hours ago were followed by the chef's presentations of our other catches of the day. My favorite was the grilled swordfish steak topped with a lemony salsa of mango and chilies.

A whole parrot fish was stuffed with whole heads of garlic and baked with orange slices and herbed butter. The ubiquitous sides of rice and tortillas seemed superfluous to me. We decided for health reasons to switch to Dos Equis beer with our meal, as a day in the sun made for thirsty hombres.

We finished the evening with flan, a *robusto* Mexican coffee spiked with Kahlúa, Cuban cigars, and *mas café*.

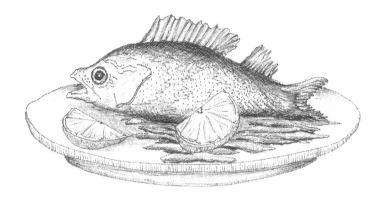

## Mango Salsa

Mango salsa makes a great topping for grilled fish, roasted pork, or chicken.

Ingredients:
2 ripe mangos, peeled, pitted, and diced
2 ripe tomatoes, chopped
1 ripe tomatillo, shelled and diced
2 jalapeños, seeded and diced
2 cloves garlic, pressed
1 medium onion, diced

juice of one lemon
juice of one lime
2 tablespoons chopped cilantro
1/2 teaspoon kosher salt
1/4 teaspoon fresh ground black pepper

Combine all ingredients in a large bowl. Mix well, cover, and refrigerate 4 hours or more.

Some prefer to add a few pinches of cumin powder for added flavor.

# Shrimp Ceviche

Ingredients:
1 pound medium raw shrimp, peeled and deveined
2 cups Mango Salsa
4 ounces tequila

Place ingredients in a nonreactive, sealable container. Mix, cover, and refrigerate at least 8 hours to allow the acidity and booze to "cook" the shrimp.

Mix before serving over crushed ice in a parfait glass with a lime wedge. This is a great start to a nice carne asada made with a couple of 9-ounce flatiron steaks marinated in *mojo*.

# Chef's Notes:

_____

_____

_____

_____

_____

_____

_____

_____

_____

_____

_____

_____

_____

_____

_____

_____

# Part 4

## *Things*

# Chapter 23

## *The Grill*

Charcoal or gas? That is the question grilling pros will argue late into the night. I have both because the arguments made by both sides are equally credible. In fact, you can buy units that go both ways.

Gas grills are more convenient than charcoal. They offer almost instant heat, quick starting, and easy cleanup, but to me, charcoal-cooked food tastes a little better. My gas grill allows me to boil and steam, but charcoal is best for slow, even heat and adding smoke. If you decide on charcoal, I recommend a charcoal chimney to start your grill instead of liquid lighter fluid because the residual chemical odors affect your taste buds.

The purchase of a new grill can be a daunting adventure. The choices out there are endless. The process is as time consuming as buying a new car and involves a lot more hand-wringing. BTUs, grid size, rotisseries, warming trays, auxiliary burners, storage capacity, controls, domes, chimney, grease traps, gauges—the combinations are endless.

Ultimately I chose a 55,000-BTU, five-burner, electric-rotisserie-equipped, four-wheeled, stainless-steel, baked-enameled-porcelain-coated, chrome-handled, four-door beauty standing over four feet tall and five feet wide and weighing in at a quarter ton! I didn't know how good it cooked, but like the '67 Corvette convertible I drove in my thirties, it sure looked good on me.

For charcoal, I chose a two-chamber domed unit that allowed for smoking and grilling with indirect heat from charcoal or wood. The pull-out ash-removal tray is a must. So are cast iron grids.

A new grill, gas or charcoal, should be thoroughly cleaned when you bring it home from the store. There's no telling what's been in it. Wash all the surfaces with warm, soapy water and thoroughly rinse, drain, and dry. Now it is ready to season.

Seasoning is the process of sealing surfaces with oils and carbon. This helps prevent rust on interior surfaces and reduces sticking on cooking grids, griddles, and racks. This is how you treated your cast iron cookware, no? Brush or spray all interior surfaces with canola oil. Fire up the gas or charcoal and close the lid. After the temperature reaches 400 degrees F, add a handful of wood chips to the heat. The resulting smoke will add more carbon to the surface coating. About an hour of high-temp seasoning, and your grill is ready to go. That cast iron cookware can be seasoned inside the grill at the same time. Multitasking: it's what cooks do.

Steaks, chops, ribs, and chicken are universal barbequing staples. Plain or fancy, rubbed or marinated, they are best enjoyed when properly grilled. Many of us don't like to have our grilling prowess questioned, feeling such criticism a threat to our manhood.

One of the toughest things to master on a new grill is heat control. Cooking the inside without burning the outside requires skill that is developed by taking information and putting it into practice. With meat costs spiraling ever upward, the trial-and-error method of polishing your grilling skills could lead to your new, expensive grill showing up at a repo auction. Read a book or two about grilling, know your equipment, and start off slowly. Master the hot dog, burger, and bun before trying to get that fifteen-dollar porterhouse medium rare.

## Marinated Chicken Breasts

Here are three marinades for chicken breasts that you may like to play with. Each is a blend of something acidic, something sweet, oil, and some herbs. You can create a hundred variations and find one to suit your tastes. Marinate chicken 3–4 hours covered in refrigerator, turning a couple of times. Always discard marinade that any raw meat has been in. I make a second batch for basting and avoid raw parts of meat with my basting brush.

Each marinade will be enough for four boneless, skinless chicken-breast halves. Season with salt and fresh ground pepper to taste before marinating.

## Sweet and Tangy Marinade

1/4 cup each soy sauce, orange juice, and honey
2 tablespoons each sesame oil and minced green onion

## Hot and Spicy Marinade

1/4 cup each soy sauce, peanut butter, and white wine
2 teaspoons each red pepper flakes and fresh grated ginger

## Southwest Marinade

1/4 cup each olive oil, lime juice, and honey
1 tablespoon each chopped cilantro and minced garlic

Citrus is best fresh-squeezed. Apple cider vinegar, tarragon vinegar, or wine vinegars make good acidic substitutes. Using a blender or food processor will allow for greater experimenting, especially if you have a Chef-ette for cleanup. Or buy one of the hundreds of meat marinades offered at your local grocery. Most are good, and some are quite exceptional.

Cook marinated chicken over medium-heat coals about 6 or 7 minutes per side, brushing on more marinade every few minutes.

Move to upper rack, close lid, and bake until meat thermometer registers an internal temperature of 165 degrees F. Some flare-ups just add more flavor to the meat.

Serve with grilled corn and a nice salad.

## Fruit on the Grill

Grilling is not just about meat on the fire. A lot of foods respond well to the effects of an open flame and heat. Fruits and vegetables with high sugar content (fructose) bloom with sweetness when properly fired. We all know about grilled corn on the cob and how potatoes are so much better with a little char, but here are three things few people think of when it comes to grilling: apples, peaches, and pineapples.

## Grilled Apples

Ingredients:
2 Granny Smith apples
juice of half a lime
melted butter

Core the apples and cut into 1/2-inch-thick rings. You can hold the cut rings in cold water and the juice of a half a lime until you're ready to grill.

Spray cooking grid with canola oil. Drain and dry apple rings. Brush with butter and grill, turning when grill marks appear.

If you overcook, rings will fall apart. These make a nice side for pork dishes.

## Grilled Peaches

Ingredients:
2 tablespoons sugar
1/4 teaspoon ground cinnamon
4 tablespoons butter
4 peaches, halved and pitted

Mix sugar and cinnamon and spread on a shallow dish.

Melt butter in small bowl.

Dip face of peach halves in butter and then into sugar mix.

Place face down on sprayed grid and cook until sugar caramelizes. Turn peach halves over and finish the cooking 3–4 min.

Goes great with chicken.

## Grilled Pineapple

Ingredients:
1 fresh pineapple
melted butter for brushing

Remove top and core of pineapple but do not peel. Cutting from top to bottom, quarter pineapple. Trim any of the missed core.

Brush flesh with butter. Roast on grill until charring and grill marks appear. Turn peel side to grill and continue cooking and basting for 3–4 minutes.

Serve with pork or fish.

# Chapter 24

## *From the Grill*

For me, there's nothing like the aroma of a steak sizzling over hot coals, flares of flame from every drop of rendered fat adding more flavor to the meat. A wire brush, a splash of cooking spray, and some heat combined with a generous amount of elbow grease before each use will help you get the most out of your grill. BBQ season is year round. As the seasons change, be sure to reseason your grill.

So now my grill is set to go, ready for another eight months of chicken, steaks, chops, roasts, burgers, dogs, veggies, and potatoes. Did I mention the steaks? This year I plan on doing more smoking on my grill and burning some wood with the charcoal. Chicken, pork loin, and spareribs are the usual suspects, but I think I'll try a little smoke on some fish, roasts, and maybe even duck. We'll see what the wind blows in, but for now, I can't get that 2-inch porterhouse out of my head.

Alas, the 2-inch porterhouse is only a fantasy, sans a bank loan. I could probably float an advance on my allowance if I ask Linda politely, but even if she pops for the necessary gilt, the ensuing guilt would take the joy out of the event. I couldn't eat the monster anyway, even with her help. We'll settle for a nice 5-ounce filet and allow room on the plate for some kind of a potato, grilled mushrooms, and maybe later, something sweet for dessert. Grill on, my friends. Grill on!

Grilling burgers will provide the same olfactory satisfaction as the most expensive cuts of beef, and I insist on treating my burgers with the same kindness and respect that I would any steak.

A good hamburger steak starts out with fresh ground beef, preferably ground chuck or, better yet, ground round. Ground sirloin might be a bit too lean, and I see no reason for grinding up a perfectly good steak. Pick out a chuck roast or a round steak and ask your butcher to grind it up for you. Don't double grind. This is the method used to make hamburger (ground beef) from the toughest of beef. Having an 80/20 or 81/19 lean-to-fat ratio doesn't mean that the hamburger consists of ground up chuck or round. Hamburger will be marked *ground round* or *ground chuck* only if it is, no matter the fat content. Pay a little more, pick out the cut you want, and have the butcher do you right. You'll see and taste the difference.

When you get home, hand form a couple of 1/2-pound patties, about 1 inch thick. Place on a platter, cover with plastic wrap or foil, and put in the freezer for an hour. What? Yes, I put them in the freezer for an hour, and here's why: How many times have burgers broken when you try to turn them on your grill or the edges split and crumbled? These thick-formed patties will handle better if you start out with them slightly frozen. It would take about four hours to freeze them through and through. I think this also keeps the inside juicy and tender while a little bark forms on the outside from the fire.

The next thing is seasoning your burgers. Sea salt and fresh ground pepper are essential, but you should know that letting salt stand on raw meat causes moisture loss, resulting in dried out burgers. You want to season the meat just before putting it on the fire. The heat will sear the meat, and the seasonings will permeate the burger. Always season the side that will face the heat first, and don't season the other side until you are ready to turn it over. I use Canadian steak seasoning on these babies, which is basically salt, pepper, and garlic, but again, the seasoning rule must be followed.

I like my burgers medium-rare (pink inside), and you must attain an inside temperature of 165 degrees F, long enough to kill any bacteria. You can do this by cooking the burgers to the desired outside doneness, 4 minutes on each side over medium-high coals, and then moving the burgers to a cooler part of your grill, off direct flame, and letting them rest for a few minutes. You have a meat thermometer, right?

## Caramelized Sweet Onions

Ingredients:
1/2 stick butter, melted
1 large sweet onion, peeled and thinly sliced
1 tablespoon chopped fresh parsley
1 teaspoon flour

Melt butter in small saucepan over hottest spot on your grill. Add onion. Sauté until onion starts to brown.

Stir in flour and parsley, cooking to thicken and darken a bit. Cover and move to cool part of grill. Reserve for plating mashed potatoes and garnishing.

You can use this same recipe for sliced mushrooms. Or why not combine the two by cooking them together?

## Parmesan Mashed Potatoes

Ingredients:
1 pound Yukon Gold potatoes, washed and quartered
2 quarts water
2 tablespoons kosher salt
1/2 stick butter
1 tablespoon fresh parsley, minced
1/2 cup grated Parmesan cheese
salt and pepper to taste

Boil potatoes in salted water until done. Drain well and return to pot.

Using potato masher, mash potatoes with skins on, adding rest of ingredients in order.

You might need a little milk if too thick. Skins and lumps add interest to this dish.

## Hamburger Steak Presentation

Heat two dinner plates. Place half the onions in the center of each plate and spread in a circle with back of a spoon.

Pile half the mashed potatoes on top of each circle, allowing a margin of sautéed onions to border the mashed potatoes.

Place hamburger steaks on top of the potatoes. Garnish with a cherry tomato impaled on a frilly toothpick. Or you could grill some mushroom caps brushed with butter and use them for a garnish.

# Chapter 25

## *Bacon*

A Father's Day gift got me thinking about bacon. Again! Fact is, we guys tend to think about bacon a lot. For some of us, there is only one thing we think about more. If you split our heads open you'd find our frontal lobes dotted with bacon bits and our cerebral cortexes wrapped in rashers of hickory-smoked, sugar-cured, thick-sliced bacon.

While a large portion of the right side of my brain is devoted to the many nuances of bacon aromas and flavors, the left side contains a couple of languages, along with a thousand ways to get more bacon into my diet. I am so bacon-centric that I can hear bacon sizzling without the help of my hearing aids, and although I can ignore an alarm clock with the best of men, the smell of cooking bacon will get me up every time.

All chefs know that the use of bacon should not be limited to including it on the breakfast plate alongside two eggs and some hash browns (the most popular use). They understand that bacon is also a condiment that enhances everything. They wrap it around things, like shrimp, scallops, filet mignon, or hot dogs, knowing bacon makes them better.

Summer is the height of grilling season, and bacon works well with flame or coals. So be creative in your use of bacon. Try skewers of apple or pear wedges wrapped in bacon slices. Spirals of chicken tenders and bacon grill nicely on a stick too. My steak kabobs hold together better when I weave a thick slice of bacon over each addition to the skewer.

Try wrapping an ear of corn in foil with a slice of bacon and giving it 15–20 minutes over medium coals, turning every 3–4 minutes for even roasting. Do the same with a baking potato; just stick your fork into the raw potato a few times before wrapping. Of course you'll need more baking time. If you're using charcoal, put your "mickeys" right on the coals; just move them around a couple of times for even baking.

I encourage all you cooks out there to remember the four basic food groups: bacon-topped, bacon-wrapped, bacon-filled, and *bacon*!

## Grilled Cabbage with Hot Bacon Dressing

I enjoy fresh cabbage, and just like turnip greens and collards, cabbage enjoys a special relationship with pork fat and vinegar. The practice of boiling up cabbage or other greens with some ham bones, pig's knuckles, or jowls has been around since shortly after the discovery of fire, and these are usually served up with a side of vinegar to give them a little kick. But this is grilling time, so I prefer to grill cabbage wedges and serve them with a hot bacon dressing.

### Grilled Cabbage Wedges

Ingredients:
1 large head cabbage
4 thick slices bacon
1/2 sweet onion, finely diced
a dash each of salt and pepper
1/2 cup apple cider vinegar
2 tablespoons brown sugar
1/2 teaspoon Dijon mustard

Wash cabbage, removing any loose leaves. *Do not* remove core. Cut into eight equal wedges.

Place wedges on grids over medium-high heat and cook until some color appears and grill marks form. Turn with spatula and cook other side. Remove from heat and cover to keep warm until serving.

Brown up bacon slices in a skillet. Remove from heat. Drain bacon on paper towels and crumble.

Return skillet to medium heat and add onion to bacon drippings. Season with salt and pepper and sauté until soft.

Add vinegar and sugar and simmer until reduced by a third. Stir in mustard and bacon crumbles.

Spoon mixture over cabbage wedges. This makes a great side for ribs, links, and chops. Grill on!

# Chapter 26

## *Bombs Away*

A recent visit to a bacon festival was a new experience for this bacon freak. Linda's lack of enthusiasm caused her to stay home. I beg you, ladies, to read the next paragraph.

Guys like bacon! There's no getting around it, ladies; your man likes his bacon, and he likes more bacon even better. He likes it with his eggs for breakfast, on his sandwich for lunch, and around his steak for dinner. He wants it on his salad, in his soup, and on his baked potato. Face it, ladies, if you want him to eat it, put some bacon on it.

There are all kinds of bacon out there, and we guys will eat most any of it, except, maybe, the faux stuff. But an extreme emergency might be cause to down that too. Personally, I prefer thick-sliced, hickory-smoked, sugar-cured bacon, but I enjoy the apple-wood-smoked American style bacon (from pork bellies) almost as well. Canadian bacon (from the pork loin) is great on a grilled cheese on rye with extra sharp cheddar. Italian bacon, pancetta (also from pork belly), is not smoked but cured with salt. I use pancetta as a seasoning for some of my sauces and use it fried and diced as a crunchy topping.

Bacon's growing popularity has caused the price of quality bacon (without artificial flavoring) to double over the past few years. Commodities traders who wouldn't know which end of the pig did what have made and lost fortunes betting on pork bellies.

Bacon festivals are springing up all over the country; California and Tennessee are just a couple of the states scheduling events. Recently the queen of the Blue Ribbon Bacon Festival was crowned while wearing a gown made of, what else, bacon! Those folks in Des Moines know how to party, treating guests with such crowd pleasers as chocolate-covered bacon on a stick, bacon-flavored cookies, bacon ice cream, and bacon-flavored beer.

I'm told over a hundred guys proposed marriage to the bacon-clad festival queen. Bacon's aphrodisiac qualities should not be underestimated. Scientists have discovered that certain chemicals produced in the making of bacon cause a neurochemical response in the pleasure centers of the brain. In her book *Sex and Bacon*, author Sarah Lewis proclaims bacon's sexiness. Thus, I have concluded that bacon is addictive. I've put down the booze and cigarettes but have drawn the line with bacon.

## Bacon Bomb Explosion

The ultimate combination of BBQ sauce and bacon makes this baby explode with flavor. You can cook it on your grill or in your oven. The oven is quicker, but grilling allows you to finish with a little smoke at the end. Use your favorite BBQ sauce and BBQ pork rub. I've included my Easy 1-2-3 BBQ Rub recipe for you to try.

Ingredients:
2 pounds ground pork
1/2 cup BBQ pork rub, divided
1 large yellow onion, diced
2 apples, cored and diced
plenty of BBQ sauce
1/2 cup crisp-cooked bacon crumbles
1 1/2 pounds of your favorite thick-sliced bacon

Preheat oven to 350 degrees F.

On a clean, hard surface, form ground pork into a rectangle approximately 8 inches wide by 10 inches long.

Top with half your rub and then spread onion and apple evenly over that. Brush on some sauce— about a half cup should do it—and add the crispy bacon crumbles evenly.

Roll into an 8-inch log. Sprinkle on the rest of the rub.

Weave bacon into a lattice about seven slices wide. Place pork log on the lattice and roll it so that overlap will cover the ends. Brush with more sauce.

Place on rack in baking dish and cook 75 minutes, basting every 20 minutes with more BBQ sauce. Remove and let stand 10–15 minutes before slicing into 1-1/2-inch-thick slices.

Pass me the corn bread, collard greens, and more BBQ sauce, please. If you opt for the grill, use indirect heating. I use the same setup with the baking dish and rack, letting the fat cook off. Cook

4 hours on a covered grill at 225–250 degrees F, basting every half hour. Throw your favorite wood chips on the coals the last hour for smoke.

## Kip's Easy 1-2-3 BBQ Rub

Ingredients:
3 tablespoons each white cane sugar and dark brown sugar
2 tablespoons each garlic salt, smoked paprika, and red pepper flakes (optional)
1 tablespoon each black pepper, Old Bay Seasoning, and ground mustard seed

This rub is best with pork, but I've used it on beef ribs and flank steak with some success. Moisten the beef with a sprinkling of Worcestershire sauce before applying the rub.

## Kip's Quick BBQ Sauce

Ingredients:
2 cups ketchup
1/2 cup spicy brown mustard
1/2 cup apple cider vinegar
1/2 cup brown sugar
1 tablespoon Worcestershire sauce
1 tablespoon chili powder

1/2 tablespoon red pepper flakes
1 teaspoon fresh ground black pepper
1/2 teaspoon hot sauce

Mix ingredients in saucepan over medium heat and bring to a simmer. Lower heat and simmer 10 minutes. Remove from heat and serve warm.

This sauce can be played with to suit your tastes. Try substituting honey or orange marmalade for the sugar. I've even tried peach preserves. How about adding a tablespoon of garlic powder or onion powder? Maybe substitute steak sauce for the mustard. Feel free to make this your sauce.

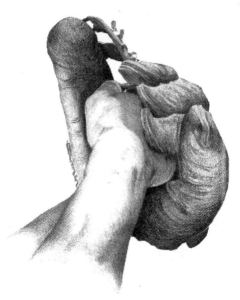

"Hey, throw me the ball!"

# Chapter 27

## *Baseball*

There was a time in America when our country set aside a week in October to celebrate the Fall Classic. The World Series of Baseball was America's premier sporting event from the beginning of the Roaring Twenties through the end of the Fabulous Fifties. I wasn't quite a year old when the first Yankees-Dodgers series was played. We lived in Nyack, a kayak ride up the Hudson from the "House that Ruth Built." Dad did "contract work" for the circulation department of the *Brooklyn Eagle*. His disposition as a player of long shots and a rooter for underdogs made him a Dodger fan.

The *Brooklyn Eagle* celebrated its hundred-year anniversary the very month that Tiny Bonham pitched the series, clinching victory at Ebbets Field and giving the Yanks the World Series Championship over the Dodgers, four games to one. Two months later, the *Brooklyn Eagle* headline read "Japs Bomb Pearl Harbor." I was fifty-three weeks old.

The Bronx Bombers and those Brooklyn Bums wound up playing five more Subway Series. The Yanks would break my dad's heart in the Octobers of my youth, beating down his Dodgers in '47, '51, '52, and, for the last time, '56, but the magical Fall Classic of 1955 was different.

In the very year the *Brooklyn Eagle* newspaper folded, the great Johnny Padres shut out the heavily favored Yanks to finally bring a World Series Championship to Brooklyn. At last, my dad, the underdogs from Brooklyn, and all those people around America who identified with their plight could celebrate. And they did. Parades, banners, flags, and personal appearances lasted through the winter. Dad bought a brand-new De Soto with his winnings—the virtue of betting long shots. He told me he would buy me one the next time the Bums won. I never got the car, and three years later, both I and the Dodgers were in California. Dad never forgave either of us.

The Los Angeles incarnation of the Dodgers became my Dodgers, and they would face the

Yankees three more times, losing in the World Series of 1977 and 1978 but winning the Fall Classic of 1981. If Dad had been alive, would he have cheered?

I'm a big fan of the chili dog. I like my hot dog grilled, not boiled or steamed, and I like my bun toasted so that the added toppings, especially chili, don't make the bun soggy and make it fall apart.

## Thirty-Minute Chili in an Hour

Ingredients:
1 pound finely ground beef
1 medium onion, diced
1 bell pepper, seeded and diced
1 clove garlic, minced
2 cups ketchup
1 cup beef bouillon
2 tablespoons dark red chili powder
1 tablespoon brown sugar
1 teaspoon ground cumin
1 teaspoon onion powder
1 teaspoon salt
pinch ground cinnamon

Brown ground beef in skillet on high heat. Remove beef from pan, reserving 2 tablespoons of pan drippings.

Reduce heat to medium and sauté vegetables until tender (5–6 minutes). Add ketchup, bouillon, and drained beef.

Bring back to a simmer and add rest of ingredients. Simmer, stirring occasionally, for about 30 minutes, which will be about an hour from the time you started. Now you have the perfect chili to put on your hot dog.

Top your dog with the chili, grated Jack cheese, and diced onions. You can kick it up by adding sliced jalapenos. Remember, you'll need plenty of napkins and cold libations to wash it down. "What's the count?"

"Willie, Mickey and the Duke"

# Chapter 28

## *Hot Dogs*

"Buy me some peanuts and Cracker Jack; I don't care if I ever get back." So the song goes, but truth be told, the hot dog is the favorite food at America's game. Hundreds of tons of them are consumed at baseball cathedrals each year. The hotdog's association with baseball led to its inclusion in the game's jargon. A player who plays with too much flair is referred to as a *hot dog*, and his style of play is called *hotdogging*. When a pitcher reaches back and puts a little extra on his fastball, he's said to be *reaching for the mustard*.

The first time I ever bought a hot dog with my own money was at a Dodgers game in Ebbets Field. It cost me a quarter, and the only choice I had was to get it with mustard or without. My bleacher seat cost half a buck, my program another quarter. Politicians hadn't invented sales tax yet, so a buck went a long way back then.

Tens of thousands of fast-food joints all over our country have hot dogs on the menu, but the vast majority of wieners are sold to American moms in supermarkets that offer a dozen brands, forcing her to decide: All meat, all beef, turkey, or a combination. Cheese? How about size? Cocktail or foot-long? Fat or skinny? How about skinless? Thus, billions and billions are consumed by us all each and every year. What do you want on your dog?

Go to a Reds game, and you'll get a Kahn's hot dog. At Dodger Stadium, the Dodger Dog is a Farmer John 10-inch all-beef frank. The Oscar Meyer wiener feeds the craving in many a park. In ballparks everywhere, some hot dog maker is vying to be somebody's "official" hot dog.

I prefer Hebrew National's all-beef franks hot off my grill, never stuck with a fork. Toast my bun alongside it and give me some mustard, relish, and onions all over the top. I avoid those healthy buns; you know the ones—whole wheat, whole grain, no preservatives. If I wanted healthy, why would I be grilling up mystery meat stuffed into animal intestines, for goodness' sake? Play ball!

How about some hot-dog exotica? We've all seen the corn dog, a hot dog on a stick dipped in cornmeal batter and deep-fried. I ran across a place that serves up foot-longs dipped in beer batter and then deep-fried and served on a rye bun with grilled onions and pan-fried sauerkraut. Absolutely wonderful. Of course, most of us like chili dogs piled high with shredded cheddar, à la the Cincinnati cheese coney, or a dog wrapped in bacon with pickles and cheese. Let your imagination be your guide. Just don't read the label.

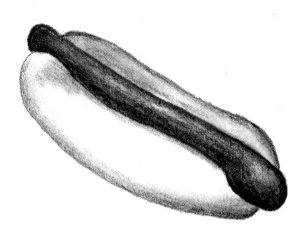

Whatta ya want on ya dawg, kid—
mustard or no mustard?

## Chapter 29

# *Dem Bums*

Any mention of Bobby Thompson's "shot heard around the world" always brings back six-decades-old childhood memories that defined my relationship with my father and my love for the game of baseball.

It was a clear October afternoon. I was a ten-year-old Yankees fan. A week earlier, my favorite team had clinched their third American League pennant in a row. However, my father was a Dodgers fan whose team had blown a thirteen-and-a-half-game lead to the New York Giants. It was October 3, 1951, and the Giants and Dodgers were playing the third game of a three-game playoff to determine the National League's champion.

The year 1951 was a pivotal one in New York baseball. Mickey Mantle and Willie Mays were breaking into the majors to dominate the next decade, both on the field and in the media. But it was to be the final year for my favorite player, Joltin' Joe DiMaggio, who would retire shortly after the World Series.

Dad was a "sporting businessman" of the Damon Runyon school who readily invested the money he made taking bets in placing bets on his beloved Dodgers. We lived in a Long Island two-story walk-up. The apartment came furnished, except for the twelve-inch Dumont television that required a huge antenna on the roof to pick up four of the five channels available to New Yorkers. The game was on, but I was outside with my "hooligan" friends, playing stickball on this, the nicest of Saturday afternoons. Dad preferred to watch the game without any Yankees fans present.

We eleven kids had formed two teams, the six Dodgers fans on one and three Yankees fans joined by two Giants fans on the other. Stickball is played on the street with a rubber ball and a broomstick. On this day, a manhole cover was our home plate, Mr. Wilson's Ford was first base, Billy Grecco's sister Angie was second base, and a telephone pole was third. Our marathon stickball game was a one-sided affair. Because Johnnie

Wilson was a twelve-year-old glandular case who weighed more than any two of us, and because his dad's car was first base, he made up the ground rules. His Dodgers stickball team was ahead 24 to 6. We members of the Giants stickball team were losing interest in shagging the rubber ball for the other team, so I ran home to get an update on the playoff game.

The Giants had won the first game on the strength of a two-run homer Bobby Thompson had hit off Ralph Branca, but the Dodgers roared back in game two to put a 10–0 pasting on the Giants. Now the Bums, to Dad's cheers and coaxing, had forged a 4–1 lead going into the bottom of the ninth inning. The promise of another chance to finally beat the hated Yankees in the World Series was making Dad giddy.

What happened in the next ten minutes would break the hearts of Dodgers fans all over the world. Many believe the Dodger manager threw the game by bringing in Branca to pitch to Thompson with the game on the line. Still others believed the Giants cheated by stealing the Dodger catcher's signs. My Dad had a different theory: a ten-year-old Yankees fan had jinxed his beloved Dodgers by coming home just in time to see Bobby Thompson hit a Ralph Branca pitch down the line and into the seats for a three run homer to win the pennant with two out in the bottom of the ninth.

"The Giants win the pennant! The Giants win the pennant! The Giants win the pennant" was Russ Hodges's famous call of the home run, immortalized in newspaper headlines the next day as "THE SHOT HEARD 'ROUND THE WORLD."

Dad chased me down the stairs, and I fell the last ten steps. "Don't come back till your mother gets home!" he yelled as I ran back to my stickball friends.

"The Giants won 5 to 4," I announced. With that, Johnny Wilson took his ball and went home, a tear running down his cheek, and Billy Grecco took second base home. It was not a good day to be a fan of "Dem Bums."

# Chapter 30

## *Things Italian*

I am often asked, "Are you Italian?" My answer often requires me to explain that my mother was born of Irish immigrants and that my father's parents were of German descent. That I became a professional cook and the owner of a couple of "Italian" restaurants often requires me to expound further.

As far back as I can remember, my favorite meal was spaghetti topped with red sauce, even if my mother made it, and she was never accused of being a good cook. My father had Italian "business associates" who owned restaurants where we would dine from time to time, and I was sure to order the spaghetti. And when Dad changed his hotel restaurant from Chinese to Italian, I was a most happy fella, with hopes of eating "real Italian" five days a week, if allowed. And so it was that I was first exposed to Italian restaurant cooking.

The new chef tolerated my presence in his kitchen and, probably at my father's insistence, even took the time to teach me enough that I would be of some use to the operation. However, his non-English-speaking mother was of a different mind.

Since not all communication need be verbal, her facial expressions, hand gestures, and occasional shoves made it clear that my inability to understand Italian was the cause of everything that went wrong. So many of the secrets of Italian cooking remained a mystery to me. I did manage to pick up a few pearls: don't overcook the pasta, and don't ever mess with Mama's sauce—*ever*. Thankfully, more learning opportunities would come my way.

## The Sauce

Ask any true Italian male, "Who makes the best meat sauce?" If his wife is not around, he'll most likely answer, "*Mama!*"

I don't know if genetics is involved or if it is sensory imprinting that creates this bias. Because

I'm not Italian, the only good thing I can say about my mother's sauce is that it was red. This meant anybody else's tasted just great to me, until I was taught better.

When Marie, my high school sweetheart and first wife, and I were dating, we went to her grandparents' summer home out on Long Island for a Sunday dinner. Quite a crowd of aunts, uncles, cousins, and friends gathered round a giant table beneath a grape arbor. I was introduced as "the boyfriend" and made to feel welcome, with a seat at the table from which I could watch the workings of my first summer kitchen.

Marie's grandmother, a white-haired lady with the brightest blue eyes I'd ever seen, was working at a very large wood-burning stove, frying meatballs in a large skillet while Italian sausages sizzled in another pan and a large pot of tomato sauce simmered on another burner. She danced from skillet to pot to skillet like a ballerina, turning this and stirring that, while conversing with her guests in two languages.

A fourth cooking pot boiled vigorously to the point of boiling over. Grandma deftly moved the foaming brew to a cooler spot above the fire and gave it a stir too. What she did next made me get up from the table and join her by the stove.

Thrusting a long-handled fork into the murky brew, she fished out one steaming pig's foot and then another and then two hocks and put them all into the pot of sauce. Standing there with my mouth open, I wondered if the eye of a newt was already in the sauce pot.

A half hour later, she handed me the fork and had me take the sausages from the pan and add them to the cauldron of sauce as she did the same with the meatballs. The best meat sauce I ever ate was but an hour away from the table. Margaret Mendolia's sauce would be the standard by which I'd measure all the meat sauces I would eat from that day forward.

Funny how we sometimes learn that many of the things we thought we knew were wrong. If we are honest with ourselves, these revelations allow us to question some other truths we have accepted over the years. I'm sure there are thousands and thousands of sauces out there better than my favorite; just ask any Italian man.

## Grandma's Meat Sauce

The following recipe is an approximation of Grandma Mendolia's great meat sauce, and in this case, close is very good.

Ingredients:
2 quarts Ginny's marinara sauce (*see chapter 12*)
1 1/2 pounds lean ground beef
1 pound sweet Italian sausages, cut into thirds
1 1/2 pounds pork ribs, cut off large end of slab
12 meatballs (*recipe below*)

Preheat oven to 425 degrees F.

Place Ginny's marinara in a heavy-bottomed stockpot over medium-low heat.

Lightly brown beef in a skillet over high heat. Pour off excess fat and add beef to sauce.

Place individually cut ribs and cut-up sausage pieces on a baking sheet, and roast in oven for 20 minutes. Add to sauce.

Add cooked meatballs to sauce. Let everything stew at a simmer for 90 minutes.

Remove ribs, sausages, and meatballs to serving platters or bowls. Ladle remaining sauce over your pasta of choice and pass the grated Parmesan. The guests will figure out what to do with the plates of meat.

This recipe will feed a large gathering of family and friends. Serve with salad, garlic bread, and soft drinks for the kids. A Chianti Classico would be the perfect wine; look for the Black Rooster.

The secret to this sauce is the pork bone, fat, and cartilage breaking down in the simmering to add body, texture, and sweetness. *Pork fat rules*!

# The Meatballs

Ingredients:
1/2 cup Italian seasoned bread crumbs
1/4 cup milk
1 pound lean ground beef
1/2 pound ground pork
1/2 cup grated Parmesan cheese
1 large egg, beaten
2 tablespoons garlic, minced
2 tablespoons fresh chopped parsley
1 teaspoon salt
1/2 teaspoon fresh ground pepper
1/2 teaspoon dried oregano leaves
1/2 teaspoon red pepper flakes (optional)

Preheat oven to 425 degrees F.

Combine milk with bread crumbs in bottom of a large mixing bowl and let sit while you line a cookie sheet with aluminum foil. Lightly spray the foil with cooking spray (a canola spray will stand up to this temp).

Add remaining ingredients to bowl with milk-soaked crumbs. Gently mix by hand to combine evenly. Over mixing will make tough.

Form into 18 golf-ball-sized meatballs and place on cookie sheet. Bake 20 minutes, turning once halfway through to brown evenly.

## Italian Secret Ingredients

Ah, gremolata! This is an Italian cooking secret few Americans, other than serious foodies, know much about. Original gremolata is a combination of fresh Italian parsley, lemon zest, and garlic used mostly as a flavorful garnish or condiment for braised meats, like lamb or veal Osso Buco, and roasted pork, veal, or lamb.

Gremolata can also be used to bring stews, gravies, and sauces to life with a quality of freshness often otherwise missing. Bisques and many cream sauces and soups benefit from a healthy pinch of this magical concoction. Steamed veggies tossed in olive oil and a scant teaspoon of gremolata will not be long on the plate. Baked potato? Sprinkle a little on top of that blob of sour cream and make that spud pop.

Cooks around the Mediterranean have been mixing citrus, leafy herbs, and Alliums to flavor their meals for centuries, ever since citrus was first introduced from the East. The Spanish might take a green onion, a sprig of cilantro, and the zest of a lime to make their version of gremolata; the French might combine shallots with oranges and tarragon; and the Greeks may use a leek with rosemary or mint to combine with their choice of citrus zest. As you can see, the mixing of an herb with citrus and a member of the onion family is done in many cuisines. Please, experiment with this recipe.

## Basic Gremolata

Ingredients:
4 tablespoons flat leaf parsley, chopped
2 tablespoons minced garlic
2 tablespoons lemon zest

You should note the ratio of herb, in this case parsley, to the other parts. Some herbs are more powerful than others and may dominate the flavors of the other two ingredients, requiring a little less herb or a little more garlic and zest. A proper balance will allow you to identify the individual flavors of all three ingredients. I like to mix in a little freshly ground black pepper and a pinch of kosher salt, depending on how it will be used.

Another secret ingredient that many cooks shy away from is the little anchovy, a fish greatly misunderstood. Six million tons are harvested from seas around the world yearly. Many think anchovies are but a bait fish, but only a tiny portion of the annual catch is used for bait. While some are used for animal feed, most are caught for us to eat. Most Americans, unless they read the labels on the thousands of items found in today's markets, don't know they're eating anchovies.

And why would food processors be putting anchovies in the products they make for us? To sell more product, of course. Anchovies contain powerful flavor enhancers that add savory qualities that tantalize our taste buds, making us want more.

Every cook should be familiar with how Mediterranean chefs have been sneaking these condiments into their dishes to make them better. The following recipes demonstrate a few of the ways both gremolata and anchovies can make a seafood, poultry, or vegetable dish wake up your taste buds.

# Roasted Peppers and Grape Tomatoes

Ingredients:
4 bell peppers (yellow and green peppers go well with the red of the cherry tomatoes)
1 cup cherry tomatoes
4 tablespoons olive oil
4 anchovy fillets
1/2 teaspoon kosher salt
1/4 teaspoon fresh ground pepper
2 tablespoons gremolata, or more

Preheat oven to 425 degrees F.

Wash the peppers and quarter, removing stems and seeds. Wash the tomatoes and halve lengthwise.

Place the vegetables into a large bowl. Toss with olive oil to coat. Spread onto a large baking sheet.

Coarsely chop anchovy fillets and sprinkle on top of vegetables. Season with salt and pepper.

Place baking sheet into preheated oven and roast 12–15 minutes.

Remove to a serving platter. Top with a sprinkle of gremolata and serve as an antipasto or as a vegetable side.

## Bagna Cauda Sauce

Ingredients:
1/4 cup olive oil
1 head of garlic
1 (2-ounce) can oil-packed anchovy fillets
1/2 stick butter

In a small saucepan, heat oil over low heat. Separate and peel the garlic cloves and add to oil. Slowly cook until cloves turn golden, about 8–10 minutes. Remove cloves from oil to cutting board.

Drain anchovy fillets of excess oil and mash with garlic cloves. Return mash to oil with butter and cook over low heat until the mash dissolves.

Serve warm as a dip with crudités, or toss with a steamed veggie, such as Italian green beans, cauliflower, or carrots. Or add lemon zest and a squeeze of juice to the sauce and spoon over grilled fish.

It's also wonderful drizzled on a sandwich of warm hard-boiled eggs, thinly sliced onion, lettuce, and tomato made on a crusty Italian bread. Slit the baguette lengthwise, slather with bagna cauda, egg slices, onion, lettuce, tomato, and cut into small sandwiches, easily dipped into more of this great stuff. You made enough for dipping, right?

## Linguine with Albacore and Bagna Cauda

Ingredients:
2 quarts water
2 tablespoons salt
1 pound linguine
2 tablespoons olive oil
1/2 teaspoon red pepper flakes
1 tablespoon capers, drained
2 (5-ounce) cans white albacore in water, undrained
1 cup bagna cauda sauce
2 tablespoons fresh parsley leaves
juice of one lemon

Bring salted water to a boil and cook linguine according to package directions. Drain, reserving a cup of the cooking liquid. Return pasta to the pot with the reserved cup of cooking liquid.

While pasta is cooking, heat oil in sauté pan. Add red pepper flakes and capers. Cook 1 minute.

Add canned albacore with liquid and simmer 4–5 minutes, until most of the liquid cooks off.

Add bagna cauda sauce and cook another 4 minutes.

Add sauce to pasta and toss with lemon juice and parsley.

Serve with Aunt Rose's garlic bread and grated Parmesan cheese.

# Chef's Notes:

# Part 5

## *Cooking for Two*

# Chapter 31

## *The Rules*

Picture a table lit by candles, soft music playing in the background, perhaps a good wine or chilled libation out for consumption, the smell of warm bread wafting all about. A menu of favorite foods should leave plenty of time to enjoy both the food and company. The picture is easy to conjure up, but what would it be without someone special to share it with? Now, I'm not talking about some family meal with the kids or a dinner party with friends, I'm talking dinner for two, a statement of love.

There are rules:

1) *Always start with a salad.* A salad says we'll start out easy, never heavy, not too sweet or too bitter. Maybe a little crunch and some color. Chill the plate and the fork. Dress it lightly with extra dressing as

a side. Sometimes simple is sophisticated. The better it looks, the better it will taste. Guaranteed.

2) *Serve warmed or toasted bread or rolls with all courses except dessert.* Maybe with whipped butter or honey?

3) *Your entrée should have balance.* Steak and potatoes, chicken and rice, burgers and fries, and so on. And take the time to warm the plate. The food will stay warmer longer, allowing for leisurely dining.

4) *Don't forget your vegetables.* Meat, starch, and something from the garden is a winning formula. Just make sure that what you're serving compliments each course. No cabbage with my steak. No mashed potatoes with my burgers. No baked beans before the crème brûlée.

5) *Finish with a flourish.* Dessert is a must, preferably with chocolate. There should always be room for dessert. If not, the entrée was too large or the foods too heavy. Please don't rush; this is not a race.

Morning coffee?

# Chapter 32

## *Red on Red*

Her hair was the color of a warm fire, with highlights of orange and gold. A splash of freckles bejeweled her checks. Her green eyes reflected the candlelight dancing on our table. Her sensuous beauty embodied an earthiness I had never experienced before. When her glossed lips smiled, my heart skipped a beat. She smelled of vanilla, cinnamon, and herbal soap. I was smitten.

I poured the wine—a French red, of course—and placed the basket of warm, crusty bread between us. I topped the gold chargers with chilled crystal salad plates covered with Bibb lettuce and frisée greens. A tomato rose centered the presentation of poached asparagus spears and a garnishment of fresh raspberries—the reddest I could find.

Her ohs and ahs played like music to my ears as we enjoyed our salads, which I dressed in a raspberry vinaigrette. Our entrée followed: a small rack of lamb served in a wine reduction and spiked with garlic and rosemary. A rice pilaf, dotted with carrots and peas, and a little mint jelly completed the plate.

We finished with a fondue of chocolate and giant red strawberries. A pot of espresso and stimulating conversation about the virtues of red were just the beginnings of a night to remember. Love: it starts with dinner for two.

## Wine Reduction

Ingredients:
1 cup pan drippings
1 cup red wine
1 tablespoon butter
1 teaspoon flour

After roasting lamb, reserve a cup of pan drippings.

Deglaze the pan with wine over medium-high heat.

Return the drippings to the pan and bring to a simmer. Allow mixture to reduce by half.

Microwave butter in a small bowl to melt and mix in flour to make a roux. Stir roux into simmering reduction and cook to thicken.

Remove from heat and set aside until ready to plate.

# Chapter 33

## *Steak for Diane*

I walked into the bank to cash a client's check that was drawn on this particular branch. While in a line marked off by red-velvet ropes on brass stanchions, I wondered if I would be lucky enough to wind up at the window with the prettiest teller. I lost yet another lottery when the man in front of me was called to her window. Now at the end of the rope, I stepped forward when the teller working the next window called out "next" for the second time. Then it got a little crazy.

The pretty teller fainted, and her customer spun around and ran right into me. I grabbed hold of him to keep from falling over but to no avail. We wound up on the floor, tangled in the velvet ropes and stanchions. Turns out the guy was a would-be bank robber thwarted by the old "fainting teller" trick. Needless to say, I was grateful he was only armed with a note. As a reward for my bravery, I was given a free checking account, which the pretty teller dutifully helped fill out, using the client's check to fund it.

Her name was Diane, and she made it a point to assist me whenever I needed a banking service, which seemed to be two or three times a week, as I attempted to hook up with her. She lived in Hollywood, only working at the bank until her big break came along. Diane made it a point to tell me that I wasn't it by spurning my offer to cook for her. She claimed to be a committed vegetarian and insisted she was very particular as to what she put in her body. Too bad, Diane, you missed out on a great dinner.

Diana, the sister of Apollo, was the Roman goddess of wild animals and the hunt. Revered for her beauty and athletic prowess, she considered her body to be a sacred temple. Hence, when a hapless hunter interrupted her bath, she shot him down—something like what the bank's Diane did to me.

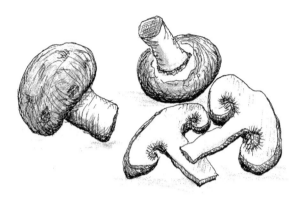

## Steak Diane

You don't have to be a Diane or Diana to enjoy this wonderful meal, although it is best enjoyed by meat lovers. Nor do you have to be a culinary artist to make my simplified version of this steakhouse favorite from the '50s and '60s.

I first saw Steak Diane prepared at New York's Drake Hotel in 1958 and was mesmerized by the cooking gymnastics of the headwaiter as he flambéed the tenderloin medallions in cognac to the ohs and ahs of the of the dining room guests.

Ingredients:
1 tablespoon canola oil
6 (2-ounce) medallions of beef tenderloin
2 tablespoons Dijon mustard

2 tablespoons butter
1/2 cup diced onion
1 cup sliced mushrooms
sea salt and fresh ground pepper
1 teaspoon Worcestershire sauce
2 ounces beef stock
2 ounces heavy cream
2 ounces brandy
1 tablespoon fresh parsley, coarsely chopped

You'll need a large flambé pan and a charcoal hibachi for tableside cooking, but an electric skillet will work just fine.

Heat oil over medium-high heat until it just begins to smoke. Spread half the mustard on one side of each steak and sauté, mustard side down, for 2 minutes. Repeat for other side. Remove medallions to a plate. Cover to keep warm.

Melt butter in pan and sauté onions until clear. Add mushrooms. Season with salt, pepper, and Worcestershire, cooking mushrooms until done, about 4 minutes.

Push contents to one side of pan. Add beef stock and deglaze pan. Now the fun part.

Pour in brandy and ignite with a match or lighter. When flames die out, return steaks and their juices back to pan, allowing to heat.

Slowly add cream to mushrooms and juices, coating the medallions with the resulting "Sauce al a Diane."

Sprinkle with chopped parsley and serve with potatoes and lemon-buttered asparagus. The gods will smile upon your table.

# Chapter 34

## *Surf and Turf for Anita*

I placed the hibachi on the center of the table and put a match to the dozen or so charcoal briquettes. I had an hour until my guest was due to arrive. It was cool for an August night, making the little table on my balcony perfect for the seduction I had planned.

I sliced an eight-ounce sirloin into thin strips and placed them in a marinating brew of teriyaki, honey, ginger, and slivers of green onion. Then I peeled and deveined a dozen large shrimp and let them swim in the juice of one lime, a teaspoon of sesame oil, and two cloves of minced garlic.

My rice steamer was loaded with a cup of white rice. For a salad I made a slaw of shredded carrot, seeded cucumber, and bok choy, dressed with just the right amounts of peanut oil and rice-wine vinegar and spiked with a teaspoon each of honey and soy sauce.

Quarter-inch slices of squash and sweet potato sprinkled with sea salt, a little pepper, and a few drops of sesame oil, were set aside to await the hibachi's heat to set their flavors free. The green tea ice cream in my freezer would be the perfect dessert.

I had the table set with rice bowls, ceramic plates of varying shapes, and tiny cups for the sake. Chopsticks added yet more charm to this effort, along with a few laughs. Paper lanterns that I had strung on my balcony provided a warm glow. I lit the candle warmer under the sake as Anita knocked on my door. How could I miss?

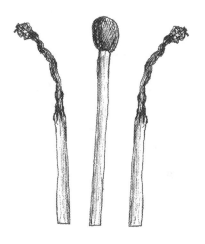

"Two down—one to go!"

# Chef's Notes:

# Chapter 35

## *Charcoal or Gas*

She knew I liked to cook, and she liked to quiz me from time to time about various aspects of cooking. I wondered if her curiosity was about the culinary arts or more personal when she asked me if I would accompany her to the local hardware store to purchase a BBQ grill.

My response—"Charcoal or gas?"—was met with a puzzled look, prompting me to continue. "Are you going to cook on a charcoal grill or one that uses propane gas?"

"I don't know, Kip. What's the difference?" she replied. This led to her accepting my invite to my place that evening for a nice dinner for two and grilling demonstration.

I stopped at the local Whole Foods and picked up some odds and ends, including fresh rosemary, corn on the cob, and a couple of small zucchini. Eight more dollars got me a handful of fresh-cut flowers on the way out the door.

She was a few minutes early, unafraid to be thought of as too eager. I poured us some wine and led her to the patio. Slices of a small tenderloin marinated next to the charcoal grill that was almost ready to roast it along with slices of squash splashed with fresh lemon and a little olive oil. Bread sat in a warm oven, ready to be torn. Earlier I had grilled the corn, cut it from the cob, and chilled the kernels. A salad of roasted red peppers and corn on crisp greens with a lime vinaigrette dressing waited patiently in the fridge.

The flowers and candlelight suited her fancy, and the Chardonnay proved to be her favorite, or so she said. K-earth 101 played some Righteous Brothers as I brought the salads and warmed bread to the table. I asked her to put the tenderloin on the grill. After all, this was a cooking lesson, no?

## Balsamic Glazed Pork Tenderloin

Ingredients:
1/2 cup balsamic vinegar
4 tablespoons olive oil

2 tablespoons brown sugar
1 tablespoon Dijon mustard
2 cloves garlic, peeled
1 teaspoon fresh rosemary leaves
1/2 teaspoon salt
1/2 teaspoon black pepper
1 pork tenderloin, about 1 pound

Place first eight ingredients in blender and pulse a few times to a froth. Divide in half.

Slice tenderloin into 1/2-inch-thick rounds. Place in flat-bottomed dish and pour half the marinade over all. Turn slices and marinate at least 30 minutes at room temperature.

Arrange slices on hot grill and roast each side approximately 3 minutes, basting frequently with marinating liquid.

Pour other half of marinade into a small saucepan and simmer over medium heat for 4–5 minutes to thicken. Spoon over plated tenderloin rounds to glaze.

A nicely chilled Chardonnay would be an appropriate accompaniment.

# Roasted Peppers and Corn Salad with Lime Vinaigrette

Ingredients:
2 ears corn, husked and washed
1/2 cup diced red bell pepper
1/2 cup diced green bell pepper
cooking spray
1/2 cup diced red onion
2 tablespoons chopped cilantro leaves
1 teaspoon sugar
4 tablespoons olive oil
juice of 2 limes
salt and pepper to taste
4–6 drops hot sauce (optional)

Cut kernels from corn cobs and mix in a bowl with diced peppers.

Spray cookie sheet with cooking spray and spread mixture evenly onto pan. Place under broiler until some charring appears. Remove and let cool.

Mix remaining ingredients in a bowl to make vinaigrette. Add corn and peppers. Mix well and refrigerate at least 2 hours to allow flavors to meld.

Serve in lettuce-leaf cups. I have added black beans to this salad to extend it. Rinse the beans and drain well before mixing. Minced garlic or chopped chives can be used to intensify flavors.

# Chapter 36

## *Midnight Repast*

We met at a friend's party, probably not by chance. Small talk over cocktails was continually interrupted by acquaintances who mistakenly thought it would be rude not to say hello and ask how things were going.

"If we are to have any meaningful conversation, perhaps we should leave," I said half-jokingly.

"Your place or mine?" I had not been expecting that response. Mine was closer. Once there, we went to my kitchen. I had a chilled Chablis waiting for a special occasion, and this seemed that it might be one.

"I'm hungry. Care for something?" I asked, making my move.

"What do you have?" she countered.

I had a loaf of great French bread, some baby spinach, eggs, and a blue cheese imported from a French cave. I put on a show and got her to help by adding a dash of onion powder to the eggs. The small galley kitchen made the act of two people cooking a contact sport. She was impressed with my pepper mill and use of sea salt. Plenty of whipped butter spiked with a pinch of fresh herbs from my window box garden really won her over.

I lit a candle for our table, lowering the lights. Barry White helped set the mood as we sipped wine and enjoyed our omelets with bread warm from the oven. We gave up on small talk when she insisted on taking care of dessert, the candlelight dancing in her eyes. I live by the Boy Scout motto: be prepared.

## Spinach Omelet with Chives and Blue Cheese

Ingredients:
4 large eggs
2 ounces half-and-half
1 tablespoon chopped chives
salt and pepper to taste
2 tablespoons butter
2 cups fresh spinach leaves, washed and dried

1/2 cup blue cheese crumbles, divided

Whisk together eggs, half-and-half, chives, salt, and pepper to a froth in a large bowl.

Melt butter in your omelet pan over medium-high heat and pour in egg mixture. Layer spinach evenly onto eggs and sprinkle on half the blue cheese crumbles. Cover pan, reduce heat to low, and cook 2 minutes.

Uncover and use a soft rubber spatula to fold omelet onto itself. Top with remaining cheese and cover. Remove from heat and let set for an additional minute.

Halve the omelet and serve on warm plates with pieces of French bread, hand torn from the baguette just pulled from the oven. Strawberry preserves and whipped cream cheese work well with the warm, crusty bread.

Omelet Tips:

The right equipment helps. A Teflon pan with curved sides, 8–10 inches wide with a fitted lid. There will be occasions when you'll want to place your pan in the oven or under the broiler, so no plastic or rubber handles.

A large bowl will allow you to whisk up a half-dozen large eggs without sloshing the mixture all over the place.

A thin wire whisk 10 inches long will allow for good aeration.

A large soft-rubber spatula works best for lifting and turning your omelet. Metal and hard plastics will scratch your pan and tear the omelet.

Nothing cooks eggs like butter, and butter does best with medium heat, which is also best for omelets. Canola oil is the next best cooking medium.

The omelet pan should be at cooking temperature before you pour in the eggs. Let the butter be your guide.

The egg mixture should set up some before you add the fillings. A lid will reflect heat back to the eggs, speeding up cooking without scalding the bottom.

Cheese goes best on the top of the omelet.

# Chapter 37

## *Don't Forget Brunch*

Brunch, the merging of breakfast and lunch, is one of my favorite things. It probably brings out the romantic in me. I'll give you some brunch rules, a little technique, and a few suggestions, both to edify and entertain. The rules may not suit you, the technique may not be your style, and you may not be prone to suggestion, but this is what works for me.

Rules:

1) Make it intimate—you and someone special. Add more people at your own peril. More than four? Do a buffet.

2) Fruit and flowers are a must. Linens, china, and crystal are nice; save the paper and plastic for your picnic basket.

3) Include juices, coffees, and teas, of course, but don't forget the bubbly. It's not just for New Year's and weddings. Brunch with your sweetie is a very special occasion too.

4) Be creative. Your menu, table setting, and location should all complement each other.

Juice? Try mixing six ounces of OJ with a scoop of vanilla ice cream and a half cup of ice in your blender to make two juice glasses of an orange frosty. Garnish with an orange pinwheel and mint sprig, and you get a "wow."

Fruit? Peaches and cream on pancakes and melon balls in white grape juice or champagne.

Eggs? There's no end to the number of different omelets you can serve up, and there are all kinds of ways to cook eggs. I usually include eggs at brunch along with a meat or two. And don't rule out fish.

Toast? Break away from the standard white or wheat sandwich slices and grab a loaf of one of those artisan breads you can find in most markets. Thick slice it and panfry in a mix of olive oil and butter in a cast iron skillet. Place on a warmed plate and top with a minute steak that you've marinated in red wine and fried in the same pan. Top with a fried egg, cooked sunny-side up, and serve. Please pass me the Tabasco sauce.

Hope you're getting the idea.

# Chapter 38

## *Sweets for the Sweet*

I started out the "Learning to Cook" section of this book with "Fire," so I must end with this section in flames. "Cooking for Two" is about sharing my love for food with someone special. The following four recipes incorporate fire, warming the soul with the romance of a dancing flame, and creating a special moment just for the two of you. Flambé on!

### Bananas Foster

Ingredients:
1/4 stick butter
1/2 cup brown sugar
1/4 teaspoon ground cinnamon
1 1/2 ounces banana liqueur
2 bananas, peeled and bias cut into half-inch slices
1 1/2 ounces rum
4 scoops vanilla ice cream

Melt butter in a flambé pan or small skillet over medium heat.

Stir in sugar and cinnamon and cook, stirring, until sugar melts.

Stir in the banana liqueur and add banana slices. Cook until the bananas soften and brown a little.

Add rum and remove from heat. Ignite the rum with a lighter and allow to burn until flames die out.

Evenly divide banana slices and syrup over two scoops of ice cream. Your dining partner will be impressed.

## Cherries Jubilee

Ingredients:
1 (16-ounce) can cherries
1/2 stick of butter
1/4 cup brown sugar
2 teaspoons cornstarch
1/4 cup brandy
4 scoops vanilla ice cream

Drain cherries, reserving juice.

Melt butter in flambé pan over medium heat. Stir in sugar. When sugar dissolves, stir in cornstarch and cherries.

Slowly add reserved juice. Continue stirring as the mixture simmers and thickens.

Stir in brandy. Remove from heat and ignite brandy vapors with lighter. When flames die down, spoon over ice cream. One bowl and two spoons might be the way to go.

The following two desserts incorporate a different sort of flame. The first requires a candle-heated fondue set, the second a butane torch.

## Chocolate Fondue

Ingredients:
1/2 cup whipping cream
1 teaspoon vanilla extract
1 teaspoon instant espresso coffee crystals
10 ounces semisweet chocolate morsels
1/2 cup caramel topping
1 shot 151 rum (optional)
fresh fruit and ladyfingers for dipping

Combine cream and vanilla in a small saucepan over low heat and bring to a simmer. Do not let come to a boil. Stir in coffee crystals.

When crystals completely dissolve, start adding chocolate morsels 1 ounce at a time while continuing to stir. Add caramel the same way.

This is great without the rum, but I found the rum makes things go a little smoother.

Transfer to your fondue pot, and light the candle. Save that electric fondue rig for cheese; this is about the flame.

Fresh fruit, like strawberries, honeydew, cantaloupe, ripe pear slices, and apple slices, makes for excellent fondue dipping.

## Crème Brûlée

Ingredients:
2 cups heavy cream
1 teaspoon pure vanilla extract
1/2 cup fine sugar
4 large egg yolks
1 teaspoon orange zest (optional)
1/3 cup light brown sugar

Preheat oven to 300 degrees F.

Combine cream and vanilla in a 2-quart saucepan and simmer over medium heat for 4–5 minutes while stirring continually. Remove from heat and allow to cool for 7–10 minutes.

In large bowl, whisk egg yolks with fine sugar to form a yellow froth. Slowly stir egg mixture into cream. A whisk will work fine for this; just don't beat.

Divide custard into four 7-ounce ramekins, filling to about a 1/4 inch from top. Place ramekins into a baking pan. Pour hot water into the pan, bringing the water level a little over halfway up the sides of the ramekins.

Place into preheated oven and bake 40–50 minutes, until the custard sets. You can check center with a knife. Blade tip should come out dry, leaving a cut in the custard.

Remove from oven and let stand 20 minutes. Remove ramekins from water and refrigerate 3 hours or overnight.

I prefer to serve at room temperature and take the crème brûlée out of the fridge 2 hours before serving.

The final step is the hardest. I sprinkle a little orange zest on top, and then sprinkle with brown sugar. Equally divide the 1/3 cup between the 4 servings. Fire up a butane torch, and caramelize the sugar to a golden brown, starting in the middle and rotating the flame outward in a circular motion. No torch? Use your broiler and watch closely.

Let the sugar crust cool before serving. Garnish with a strawberry fan or an edible flower, and see where it gets you.

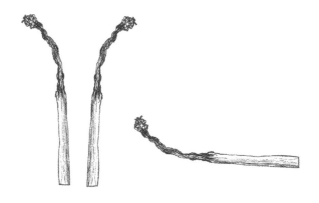

"Three down—time to go!"

# Chef's Notes:

_____

_____

_____

_____

_____

_____

_____

_____

_____

_____

_____

_____

_____

_____

_____

_____

_____

_____

_____

_____

# Acknowledgments

It takes a lot of guts to assume that others might be entertained and enlightened by my personal stories. I have written about a life filled with characters because I believe they deserve to be remembered. That you can't find your name in any of these stories only means you are still alive.

I feel compelled to give a shout-out to a few of the living who have made significant contributions to this effort. Among these is Clay Warnick, editor of the *River Times*, who has encouraged my writing. I thank him for providing me with a platform and forgive him for the wounds inflicted by his blue pencil.

The assemblage of all the parts could not have been done without the keen mind of my grandson, Brandon Meyerhoff. He bravely sorted through thousands of words, notes, electronic files, and published memories of an "old man" whose failing eyesight has delayed this project for years.

The art found between the covers of this book is the work of the talented artist James Reeves. His multimedia interpretations of life have entertained me for years. Jim can be reached at jim@reevesgallery.com.

Of course, I offer a special thanks to the professionals at iUniverse who helped me get this written so that a reader might understand what I was trying to say.

Most importantly, I wish to thank my reason for living, the love of my life, Linda. Why else would I do what I do?

Warm and fuzzy

# Index

Let's make a soup

Printed in the United States
By Bookmasters